WHITE EAGLE ON
LIVING IN HARMONY
WITH THE SPIRIT

White Eagle on
LIVING
IN HARMONY
WITH THE SPIRIT

WHITE EAGLE PUBLISHING TRUST
NEW LANDS · LISS · HAMPSHIRE · ENGLAND
www.whiteaglepublishing.org

First published July 2005
Reprinted with corrections October 2010

© The White Eagle Publishing Trust, 2005

British Library Cataloguing-in-Publication Data
A catalogue record for this book is available
from the British Library

ISBN 978-0-85487-158-2

Typeset in 11.5 on 15pt Baskerville at the Publishers
and printed by National Press,
Amman, Jordan

CONTENTS

Publisher's Note

WHITE EAGLE ON LIVING IN HARMONY WITH SPIRIT is a compilation of extracts from White Eagle's teaching, given over many years. In a very few cases, short passages have appeared in other printed books by White Eagle.

In this book, frequent use is made of the term 'brotherhood', and sometimes of 'the Elder Brethren' and 'the Brotherhood of the White Light', terms which are used respectively as a quality of being and as a community of souls, incarnate and discarnate. In the absence of another single word which carries the same qualities but is broader and more obviously gender-neutral, 'brotherhood' must stand not only for beings of both sexes, but those from other than the human levels, both angelic and of the natural world. The concept of this Brotherhood is a key feature of White Eagle's teaching.

Introduction

THIS BOOK is for all those who are seeking actively to work in harmony with spiritual principles. It is for those who wish to live more harmoniously, courageously and with more awareness, and it is for those who wish to bring balance and peace to their individual lives, and to the world, and thus to enable their soul's growth and the divine evolution of humanity.

Scientists discover natural laws operating throughout the physical universe. White Eagle, by contrast, describes a higher system of 'laws'—divine laws—that also govern our lives, of which we can be largely unaware. Indeed the word 'law' is limited by earthly understanding, and White Eagle's teaching gives a much broader picture than might be supposed of what divine law really means for us all.

Divine laws are eternal and omniscient and, like earthly laws, the keeping or breaking of them has consequences for us all. However, they are not only designed to protect, but also to enable. Divine laws are not merely a passive system, but they constitute *the working fabric of the universe*. They govern our lives, and they shape them, and they apply to the whole of life.

In White Eagle's teaching, five such laws are defined. The first, Reincarnation, is only incidentally covered by this book because White Eagle's account of the many lives we live is sufficiently different from the commonly-held view to merit a separate book. The other laws are Cause and Effect, or karma; Opportunity; Correspondences; and Compensation, which is sometimes referred to as the law of equilibrium and balance. Underlying them all is the law of Love, to which White Eagle's account always returns. In describing how spiritual law operates, he deals with such subjects as freewill and destiny, the meaning of suffering, the power of nonresistance, and what true acceptance is. There is much in this book about why cataclysmic events, ones that affect huge numbers of people and often lead them to question the love of God, occur. White Eagle not only shows how the divine laws further the spiritual plan for our lives, but also helps us understand how to work with them to bring healing on all levels, both for ourselves and for our world.

If you ever have wondered about the purpose of your life, or been concerned that things seem to be out of control, then reading this book will bring reassurance. In addition, it might give you the kind of understanding that can be transformational.

I

The Divine Plan and Spiritual Law...

...in All Religions

WHATEVER religion you study, whether on earth or in higher spheres, you will find the same precise law. Ultimately it is this: God is infinite and is with you, in you, guiding you, leading you (even if it is over a rough path).

God is leading you in the right way because God is divine law. *Love is divine law. Divine law is love.* This divine law of love—cohesion, a drawing together, a uniting, a unification of gases forming matter, forming eventually into an apparently solid planet—brought the whole universe into being. The planets have been formed by thought, by mind, by divine law. Life is established on the planet by the divine mind and by the human soul, and the law. The spirit of the Son of God within the soul grows and progresses by divine law. All are guided and governed by one law of harmony, love and perfection.

All scriptures contain the same truth, whether you look at the Bhagavad Gita, the Koran, the book of Hermes or the four gospels of the Christians. Why? Because truth is divine law, the law of the universe; and as it was in the beginning, so it is now—and so it shall be, world without end. It does not matter what language you speak. Water or air may be called by many names, each according to the language of your country, but it makes no difference to the element. God is within man and woman, God is within everything. Humanity cannot be separated from God—not at any time. Ascend the heights of heaven and God is there; descend into the depths of hell and God is there.

In the very beginning, great teachers or 'Sun-beings' came to demonstrate to the young souls who were just coming into incarnation from the astral world what could be achieved in the physical life if they always applied the law; the law of love, the law of harmony. These early students were learning, as you are learning today, to apply natural law to their own living, and these truths, which have been taught by spiritual teachers ever since, are known as the Ancient Wisdom. The law has been given to the great Initiates of all time, not only to Moses, not only to Jesus, but to many other great teachers, to help men and women consciously utilize the gifts of God and live in perfect harmony with these cosmic and natural laws and with the elements.

In a parable, Jesus spoke of the servants of the Master being sent into the vineyard at different periods to teach the people, who stoned and rejected the servants.* This parable has been interpreted as referring to the different teachers who came to humanity at stages of the world's evolution, until at last the earth children rejected them and they were withdrawn. There are records to be found

*Matthew 21 : 33–42.

in many places in both East and West, telling the story of the Sun–beings.

God has never left humanity without a witness; there always have been and always will be what we can only describe as human beings who stand on the peaks. Look out across the earth with us and see the masses of souls; some are toiling in darkness, some have their faces lifted; others have climbed a little way up; others are high upon the mountain. On the mountain peaks we see the Shining Ones, looking with compassion upon humanity. They, by their own effort and aspiration (combined with the blessing and the help of their Creator) have learned how best to serve their Creator and other human beings. From the mountain heights they direct rays of love (which is light) into the darkness of the earth.

With regard to the outworking of spiritual law, we like to think of life not as cut and dried: we do not put life, evolution, and progress in watertight compartments. We do not like a row of little bottles on a shelf, all neatly labelled. Universal law is cohesive, and all things fit into place, but in a way impossible for the human mind to conceive. Only the Divine Mind can fit all things into place—in its own divine manner. Do not try to be too precise in your comprehension of spiritual truth. You will never confine it in watertight compartments. You must recognize that divine law is perfect, harmonious, and all works together for good; but not as the human mind desires. This is like trying to separate grains of sand on the seashore. You must take spiritual truth as a whole, and know that all works together harmoniously. We impress upon you the need for following the light in your own heart; and do not always think that there must be better flowers in the next-door garden. Follow the light in your own heart, for it is a sure guide.

...in Every Aspect of Life

In the beginning of human life on earth, a great truth was directed onto the planet. It came in the form of the Light ... what you know as the light of men and women's hearts. It is indescribable. We cannot tell you what it is; it is for you to become aware of it, to realize it. Having realized it, you will draw your strength, your light forever more, from its true source. It is the Son. It is the spiritual Sun that the Ancients worshipped, a worship that earthly-minded people have mistaken for worship of the physical form of the sun.

The sun, the circle, is the universal circle of life; the cross, the incarnation, is the coming of spirit into matter. It is the suffering involved through the descent of all creation from the spheres of light into the darkness and density of earth, and physical matter. At the heart of the circle of life—at the very centre—is the rose; the rose which the ancients knew would bloom upon that cross, when the cross had been opened wide, expanded, surrendered, to the light of the Son of God. When that cross touched the light, then into those four arms would flow the light of the Son of God, whom you call Christ.

That same life would bloom as the rose. It would cause the rose of human experience to burst into flower. Millions are unaware of their potentialities. They are like little brown seeds buried in the earth, but within them there is the potential rose—that rose which can only grow to its full beauty of colour and form and perfume through experience, through feeling the stimulation of the forces in the earth. These earth forces cause the seed to burst and the root to grow. Such birth is usually a painful process, but eventually the rose turns its face towards the sun. Without the sun's rays it could never attain colour, perfume, or form.

The rose, then, is the symbol of triumph. The spiritual rose lies within every human being, but before that rose can blossom, the individual is stretched upon the cross. Need it be a cross of suffering? Not necessarily; it may be a cross of glory. But at the heart of the cross, the rose has ever to bloom—it cannot fail, because a cosmic law decrees that it shall bloom. Certain conditions of human life are the soil and the elements that produce the rose.

Humanity chose that path, not so much through falling from high estate, but through descending from the heavens into the state of physical form in order to fulfil a destiny. Through that path, the unconscious God in men and women will attain God-consciousness. We prefer to regard the cross as one of experience rather than of suffering. If the attitude of men and women towards physical experience is one of glorification, there opens a clear path of triumph by and through the cross, rather than of suffering.

It is true that there is suffering when the individual spirit enters matter. The instinct remains strong ever after for the spirit to be liberated, to be freed into a world of light and beauty. The soul must come into matter again, again and again in order to gain mastery over that plane of life. For this reason, you will find in every religion, all through the ages, this symbolism of the crucifixion of some particular saviour and then the resurrection of that being into the life immortal. This truth was clearly demonstrated when Jesus was crucified. The story of the crucifixion told in the esoteric gospels intimates that Jesus was not there when his body was crucified. He had already withdrawn from his body. He was seeing the whole thing from a distance, in clear and right perspective. This is just what human kind as a whole has to learn to do, and what you individually must learn with regard to your own problems and troubles. You must not allow yourselves to be drawn in, crucified and tortured. You must rise above trouble and see it rightly, dispassionately. Then the very atoms of the earth will be raised, and illumination and beautification will come to this physical planet. So remember: when you come up against harsh and cruel things, they may be your crown of thorns, eventually to lead you to resurrection and redemption.

For it is while you are on earth that opportunities are given to bring the Cosmic or Christ-consciousness through into life—and that consciousness *must* be brought through. Special opportunities are presented to men and women in their outer form to develop and grow in this God-consciousness. This is the reason why people, when they first lose their physical body and awaken to a heavenly state of consciousness (perhaps after passing through vicissitudes in the 'underworld'), see how they have neglected the opportunities afforded by the earth life. That is when the soul feels an urge and desire to return again to earth, where fresh opportunities await it.

Many say, 'When I get to heaven I shall not want to come back to earth—I don't see any need to do so'. No, you do not see the need now, but when the soul catches a glimpse of the glories of God's life, God's heavenly manifestation, God's beauty—when the soul is able to look into its inmost depth and see the potential beauty and good therein—then the soul desires only one thing, which is to purify and perfect itself.

There is nothing before you that you need fear. Look at your life on the physical plane. You have had difficult times. You have had anxious times. You have been through sorrow. All these experiences pass. God is all love and God is merciful and kind. If you come up against a law, you must obey that law. You have to obey physical law. If you refuse to obey spiritual law, you suffer. When you come to the spirit world, you have only to be carried forward, obeying God's law, loving God, loving your neighbour, and loving your surroundings. Love is the key into the glorious, heavenly bliss to which every soul is destined to pass.

Jesus said, '*Not a sparrow falls to the ground without your Father, and even the very hairs of your head are all numbered*'.* All

*A paraphrase of St Matthew 10 : 29–30.

your need is known, whether it be physical or spiritual, and everything which happens to you has a purpose. If you could see a diagram of life as it can be seen in the Halls of Wisdom in the spirit world, you would see a most intricate crisscross pattern—innumerable little lines crossing and crossing again and again, backwards and upwards, forwards and across, up and down—a most amazingly intricate plan. These little fine lines have a purpose, and all is moving according to divine law.

You must have seen for yourself how one thing leads to another. You say: 'If I hadn't met old Bob yesterday, he would not have told me to go to such and such a place; and then I should not have linked up with someone who has proved to be of the greatest importance in my life'. You all know that these things happen. You all know how you are brought to meet certain people, and to come to the right place at the right time. Because God knows your need, His–Her messengers are sent to guide and help you. Every single detail of life is watched over and cared for.

And the freewill that souls have on this journey—how much freedom do they gain? In spite of the law of destiny, which contains the overall plan of their lives, they can do little runs backwards and forwards. If you take your dog for a walk, it is free to make many little excursions here and there, but in the end it follows its master or mistress. If the dog takes too many runs, it may take it a long time to finish its walk, but it must do so eventually. So it is with men and women.

The Fall

When we tell you there is no such thing as an accident in God's universe, you may ask why God permitted such a tremendous accident as the Fall. In our school of wisdom, we look upon our Creator and the plan as being omnipotent. No human being has any power to upset the Divine Plan. Some may regard great cataclysms, such as the legendary sinking of Atlantis (said to be due to the lack of equilibrium between the forces of good and evil), as accidents. This is not so; God does not allow the universe to slip out of His or Her hands like that. There could not be anything outside the will of our Father–Mother God. What has been known as 'the Fall of Man' is a cosmic event created for the evolution of the child of God. It brings about an awakening, a realization of the soul's power to choose for itself: a realization of its freewill.

All the dark conditions and inharmonies of earth are really for human benefit. You may not see it in this way, but nevertheless when the spirit was first breathed forth from the heart of God, it descended through many planes of light and beauty in a state of unconsciousness. While still unconscious of itself as an individual, it came down to the plane of earth and took upon itself a physical body in order to develop consciousness of God within. There are these two aspects in all of you, as we have said many times: the good, the pure spirit that longs all the time for God, and the other side, enveloped in the fleshly personality, which also is striving for self-expression and that which it calls freedom. Until it learns to attune itself harmoniously, or rather surrender to the pure Spirit of God (which in reality is working with it all along its path of spiritual evolution)—until this material nature of men and women learns to work harmoniously with the Christ Spirit—it is going to suffer in the material life.

There is in every man or woman the spiritual or divine urge; and there is also that part called the mind, which seems ever at war with the spirit. Good and evil are like two wheels at work, the higher and the lower, and as yet they are not one. The higher is brought into being through the lower path of suffering: suffering, which is destined to produce finally the perfect picture, the perfect Christ-being. We tell you that all shall be raised up to the Son, shall be one with the radiance of the Sun.

This being the purpose of life, never grumble at any experience which comes to you; regard that experience dispassionately, and realize that you have something to learn from it; look ever for the lesson lying behind. Thus we would have you regard the Fall as a process of evolution, and not a violation of the Divine Plan of progress.

The soul is not sent down to this dark world of dense matter in order that it might *suffer*. Understand that. You are all well acquainted with suffering. Indeed, many of you know little else but pain and suffering. For this reason, the soul becomes enveloped in shadow and depression, and wearily longs to escape from its prison-house of flesh. If you could see more clearly, you would begin to understand that matter itself is what in a sense is called evil. The real purpose of so-called evil or darkness is to bring forth good. Out of evil comes good. Out of darkness comes light. In the beginning there was darkness; also, in the beginning, God said, '*Let there be light!*'—and there was light.

We would stress the point that nothing happens outside the plan. We mean, there is no question about this; the disciple knows that the things which come are all for the good. See good always; know that *good* is working out of the difficulties in which you find yourself. We stress this point, because we know there are some of you suffering through a karmic condition, which you have decided to wade through. You will get through … *you will get through*. Do not lose your vision that God is good: 'Not what I want, but what Thou wantest, O God!'.

Choosing for a Purpose—No Such Thing as Chance

This brings us to an all-important problem. People ask, 'What is the use of sweating and struggling and striving when, despite it all, there is so much suffering in the world?'. 'No-one has troubles like mine!'. 'Were I in a different position, I would do so differently; had I more money, I would do so much good for others'. 'My brother or sister has the money, but he or she does little with it, compared with what I would do!'.

Life being governed by law, you find yourself in exactly the place and with the very circumstances which you yourself have chosen. 'But that is rubbish!', you say; 'the choice was none of mine'. So speaks the outer self.

The real self, the divine urge, knows what you need to the last detail. Think of the God-urge as a radiant light ever guiding your soul on the path. Not a moment of your time should be wasted. It is not what is happening to you on the outer planes, not your circumstances, not the riches which you have or have not—but only your relationship from within to all beings and to God—your inner reaction to those circumstances—which is the all-important thing, and which is actually a form of initiation through which you are passing daily. Life is worthwhile, very much worthwhile, hard and bitter though it seems; set the bitterness against what you learn, what you are absorbing, and you will see that it is indeed worthwhile.

This is the law: like attracts like. You cannot escape, and it is not easy, we know: for the flesh is very heavy. It is of the earth, earthy, and it holds you. This happens only to make the spirit within you grow stronger, only to force the growth of this divine presence, this divine life that is within. Here is the purpose of the sorrows and the heaviness that you endure. You may not see the result of your efforts to rise, but does this matter if the light within is growing brighter? You are then burning up all the unwanted dross. It is the outworking of a perfect spiritual law.

Let us visualize the sun, the centre of your solar system, the spiritual Sun invisible behind the sun, and the spiritual rays descending upon humanity working in the most beautiful and wonderful way to get through into the consciousness of all the divine glory of their true being: rays working, blending, harmonizing. No matter what apparent disruption occurs on the physical plane, the rays are permeating, drawing together the threads, and weaving a glorious rainbow of colour and beauty throughout creation. Ultimately, the colour and beauty resolves itself back again into that perfect light, the Great White Light. We show you a plan where there is no such thing as chance, no such thing as accident; everything works in perfect law, under the direction of the great spirits at the head of the Seven Rays which permeate humanity.

Nonresistance

What awakens and quickens the divine spirit in the human being? The answer is simple. It is human experience—and largely that of pain and suffering. In the past, people have associated their suffering with what they have called evil. Now evil is a form of unevolved life, and it has an appointed purpose. It is used in the great plan of evolution in order to stimulate and bring to life the God-consciousness in the mortal being.

The biblical saying, *Resist not evil**, is great and wise. It means that humans should live harmoniously towards life. In not resisting evil, they may recognize the definite purpose in life that the so-called evil has. Whether it is universal or individual, evil is a force that helps progress; and without evil, life would become static. The influence evil has upon life is ultimately a good one, one which is bringing about nothing less than perfect creation. Therefore, not to resist evil

*Matthew 5 : 39.

means to recognize evil as a necessary factor in evolution.

You are beginning to understand evil when the innermost part of your being allows it to go its natural way and burn itself out. Meanwhile, instead of being caught up, that innermost part remains with its consciousness fixed entirely on the All Good. This you do when you live harmoniously, when you so take hold of your life that little things cannot master you. For it is when those little things are in charge that you yourself get worked up into a state which itself contains evil. Focus your whole being upon the goodness of God, the mind of God, on all good, positive thought. Then you do not recognize the disturbance around you. You do not resist or attack; you concentrate your whole being on all good, thus living in harmony and accord with divine laws.

Evil is always present in the world; and there are times when it seems to be particularly apparent. At such times, it wakes humanity up. To the individual, it brings a realization that there is something wrong in his or her life. If life went along without such awareness, with the evil unnoticed, still more evil would be created through that passive acceptance. Evil that becomes apparent is therefore good, because men and women then awaken to recognition of their need.

How, then, should you respond? We answer that the person seeking God should focus his or her whole being upon the light—not for the sake of self, but for others on the path. When a person feels for a brother or a sister, he or she is in a sense taking on the suffering of humanity.

If human kind did not need the light, there would not be wars and chaos. When they face this aspect of life that we call evil, men and women are hungry and thirsty for the light. Therefore, all those who turn to the light in themselves should recognize what is taking place. However slightly, they are taking upon themselves the karma of their brother or their sister. It is because the light was so strong in the Master Jesus that he took upon himself the sufferings of the world—because he could recognize humanity's need for light. Because the light in you indicates what your brother or your sister is lacking, you must feel for that other person, and so you must necessarily take on his or her karma.

We have heard it argued that in certain circumstances there is nothing to do except to fight. From a material point of view, this may be right, but from a spiritual viewpoint it can never be right. To fight is always, *always* a violation of the law of Christ. There is only one way to receive love into human life, and that is to give love forth. When there is violation of the law of love, then suffering, conflict and pain will result.

Let us take an example. In the story of Jesus in the Garden of Gethsemane,* Peter obviously had not understood the inner meaning of all the Master's teaching, or he would never have raised his sword to defend the Master. Some will say at this, 'But you could not see an innocent man murdered without attempting to kill the

*The story is to be found in St John's Gospel, chapter 18. See also St Matthew, ch. 26, and St Luke, ch. 21.

murderer!'. A difficult problem, is it not? Yet the power of love is supreme; and if this power is positively sent forth from the soul, that power will be the stronger. We mean by this that if an innocent soul was being attacked, then the power of love that flowed, shall we say, from a White Brother or Master of the Light, could protect that soul. The world may not believe or accept this statement, but we make it without reserve. When Peter broke the law of love, he broke down the light and the protection that was gathered around the Master and the disciples. Then the Master Jesus was arrested and the disciples scattered.

Jesus said to the soldiers, '*Whom seek ye?*'. When they answered, knowing what was in their minds, he replied, '*I am he*'. Jesus was thus surrendering himself, submitting to the law. Yet notice that in accordance with the law of love, the soldiers fell back—they could not lay hands upon him, because he was acting within the law of love. By saying, '*I am he*', Jesus was fortifying, protecting himself, building around himself the protection of the White Light. What broke through that great White Light which encircled him? It was Peter raising the sword against another human creature.

Telling Peter to sheathe his sword, Jesus then says, '*The cup which my Father hath given me, shall I not drink it?*'. That was an act of surrender. Jesus did not want Peter, or anyone, to enter into conflict on his behalf. He accepted that his mission on earth was finished and it was time to go hence. Here is another lesson—to accept those things that come into your life and cannot be avoided, for it means that they are your karma. Such acceptance is another great test, another great mystery. Yet you will find that the wise and the initiated always bow to the will of the divine.

All things work together for good to the man who loves God.* So, if you look for what you think is evil, you will see it, and it is very ugly; but if you gaze from your lookout above, onto what seems to others to be dark and evil, you will see that it is life in a process of evolution. Pain and suffering may be inflicted by one soul upon many souls, but presently you are astonished to see that what formerly appeared to be evil was in reality a power set in motion to bring about knowledge and good, to give people a wiser power of selection, discernment and discrimination.

We were once asked a profound question: 'What happens about the higher self of people who do truly wicked things in this incarnation? Have they still a higher self in the heaven world?'. In answer, we would say that with regard to those things that people do, you can only see the suffering caused by what is evil; but the soul which causes that suffering does not necessarily know that it is doing wrong. You will say, 'Oh, but it *must* know'. But you also know well that much argument can make black look like white. That is just what the soul of the wrongdoer does. It disguises from itself the horror of what it is doing; it can even think that it is doing something for the ultimate benefit of others. So what we would tell you is that while the process is going on, the soul is completely cut off from its higher aspect. The higher self is for that

*Romans 8 : 28.

moment a part of the being that simply cannot reach the part that is so immersed or entangled. As simply as we can put it, that is the answer: that the 'sinner' is cut off during that period from the higher self.

This is another reason why it is wise to remember how impossible it is for any finite mind to judge the evil intent of another soul, in spite of appearances.

God is all love. His–Her ways are gentle and kind; and if the soul is willing to open to the love of God, it will be filled with all blessings. If the soul is rebellious and blind, then it bangs its head against the cosmic wall—for there is such a thing. The soul must learn meekness, acceptance, humility, peace—all these are qualities of the Christ mind—but not necessarily the hard way. We have said that the soul can, if it will, learn much through happiness and joy, beauty and plenty. But if the lessons are not learnt, then these things are taken away and the soul learns through the lack of them.

God has given you freewill, and you have to be tested how you will use that freewill. You are tested many times. You may be confronted by what appears to be evil, but when your eyes are opened, you will see that what you thought was evil was only good; because you were being tested—the strength of your spirit was being tested. God does not lead you into evil, but you need God's protection, when in the presence of the tempter. You ask for God's protection, you ask that you may have your eyes opened so that you recognize all good, all wisdom, all love, and that you may abide in God.

What is Happening in your World?

To the ordinary man or woman, life usually seems chaotic. There are so many problems in earthly life that the human soul cannot answer. Yet we tell you, continually, that perfect laws control even mortal life, and that from the highest to the lowest all is law and order. So when you look at your world, and you do not understand why it is chaotic, we would once more assure you that when you enter the garden of truth, the garden of the spirit in your true home on those higher spheres, you know that all is well.

Some of you, however, have reached the point of knowing instinctively that there must be a wise purpose behind apparent chaos. You do not understand the Law, but intuitively you have felt this truth. You say, 'Yes, there is a wise purpose, and one day we shall understand it. At present we cannot understand why God not only seems to permit, but apparently inflicts, so much suffering upon innocent victims'. Beloved ones, you have taken a great step forward on the evolutionary path when you can truly say, 'There is a purpose'. As soon as you can recognize this, you are coming within the vibration of truth. Truth may not be revealed to you yet, but you are responding to the vibration of that fundamental law of the Cosmos.

When you get despondent about world affairs, tell yourself not to be silly, but to remember that God knows better than you do, and better than anyone else. If things appear to be turning topsy-turvy, hold fast to this truth and know that God is working His–Her purpose out. While there may be suffering, there will ultimately come greater happiness, far greater and more widespread than before.

We want you to know these things. We want you to get a wider vision of the present condition of the earth. When we say that we can see a possibility of peace coming in one situation or another, we mean it, and we *do* see it. We would lead you on in hope, in joy. Cannot you see that we endeavour to lead you onwards, always, so that you follow the right-hand path of light. You must ally yourselves with the forces of God and the good, and leave that which is of the left-hand* side alone. Hold in your heart a consistent thought of God's love; in spite of all bodily suffering; know that God is working out a plan far wiser and grander than any that human being could conceive. Cannot you have confidence in your Creator, and trust in His–Her love?

So we would have you think of life as one great experience in which even disharmony and suffering have their place. Vibrations playing upon the earth and upon the human soul have one divine purpose. There is no such thing as chaos in the universe. The Law is exact and perfect and all works together for good. The man or woman who will receive the greatest good must learn to accept all that comes with thanksgiving and joyousness; and the

*In traditional occult symbolism, often used by White Eagle, the true path is seen as the right-hand one, leading upwards, while the left is the one to be avoided, leading downwards.

deeper, the more shattering the experience, the grander the ultimate reward. You are privileged to be living in these days, although there are many who would prefer a quieter and more peaceful time. But these are days of great awakening, great spiritual force and power; the angels of Mars* bring to human life the creative fires to create a New Age, a new world. Great progress is being and will be made; the old structures must fall, must be broken down. Remember that all are under the Law of Cause and Effect, and no harm will come to those who are to serve and to live to see this Age ushered in. Their souls cannot be touched; their bodies will be enfolded and encircled by a ray of light. Nothing can penetrate nor destroy the physical vehicle chosen to be used as an instrument by God in the great work of laying the foundation for the building of the Temple of the New Age.

*This teaching was given originally during wartime. White Eagle's perspective on the angels of Mars is positive, for he sees them as responding completely to the law of Divine Love. For angels of both light and darkness, see another White Eagle book, WALKING WITH THE ANGELS (W.E.P.T., 1998).

II
The Law of Karma

Explaining the Law

LIVING IN some heavenly state before birth—a state of which it can remember nothing by the time it is enfolded in the flesh—every soul is instructed by angel beings as to its particular need in the incarnation to come. It is shown several possible paths. In that high state of consciousness, the soul selects its parents and the life it will live on earth. It knows full well that it will probably suffer physically, mentally, and spiritually. It is also given the opportunity so to live that if it prefers, it is able to store up its karma for the future.

Every soul may from time to time choose an incarnation that will cause it to delve into materiality and squalor. For this reason you cannot judge anyone. You do not know what great soul may dwell in some lowly body; nor can you know the reason for the choice of that particular life-experience. An advanced brother or sister, for karmic reasons, may choose to descend into the depths in order more quickly to rise to higher estate. Another soul may appear to have an easy life, enjoy material wealth, suffer no sorrow, be apparently free to travel and study and enjoy all the beauties of the earth; and yet to your eyes this one may not appear to be an advanced soul.

You may say, 'Why should so and so possess all these things and yet seem to be selfish and crude?'. Perhaps that soul has in the past stored up good karma; while it may not be very advanced, it may have a credit stored in what we call the karmic bank, credit which it elects to spend or use in one particular incarnation. Or the soul may use this karma to reincarnate in a very powerful and forceful personality. Through such an experience there may be the possibility of danger and suffering, but the individual has chosen its path, knowing full well the price that it will pay for wrong use of opportunities.

Men and women return, too, to conditions in the physical world which they have previously created for themselves. We know this will immediately cause questions to arise, such as, 'Why should I come back to such a state of life?'. 'Why cannot I remember my past life?'. 'Why should I have to suffer, when I do not know why I am suffering?'. 'How is it that I seem to be weak and unable to discipline or control myself and order my life better?'. 'Why is it that my neighbour is strong and can do all the things that I want to and cannot?'.

They are the questions which so quickly arise in the *lower* mind as soon as the angel comes to teach and awaken the soul to spiritual truth. Many today are so quickened and awakened that they know intuitively that they have lived before and accept the fact that they have earned whatever problem, difficulty, or hardship faces them—even in themselves, in their own character, as well as in the outer circumstances of their lives.

The law of karma governs the whole of life, and is by no means always bad, for while you are paying off debts you incurred in the past, you are also offered opportunities of transmuting your karma. The soul at a certain stage on the path of spiritual evolution is enabled to see its past debts and credits. The soul maybe recognizes certain people who have injured it in the past. Although they have previously inflicted injury, they do not seem to pay back any good karma in this subsequent life. But the soul thus afflicted is again absorbing and storing up good karma by its attitude and the compassion of its response.

Karma is not Punishment

Divine law operates throughout human existence. Yet we would like to put an angle upon the idea of karma that is different from the view of it as a sort of punishment meted out for misdeeds. God is Love, and the cry of the man or woman, or even of the child, is something like this: 'If God is love, why does He–She permit this suffering or that catastrophe?'. 'Where is God, to permit this terrible war?'. 'Why does God allow little children to suffer, to be ill-treated and starved?'.

Men and women have to witness the suffering of those they love, and to suffer themselves. At times they feel resentful, perhaps when they see a beloved relative or friend suffering, or maybe passing on at the most promising time of his or her life. They naturally question the love of God. And today, looking across the world and seeing the bloodshed and the suffering, there rises from the heart of the compassionate man or woman a great cry, such as we have described.

Pause with us and think. God is Good—the word 'God' *means* good. God is continually, every moment, revealing to men and women in their hearts beauty, and a feeling that is indescribable, one of ecstasy and gratitude. There is not one soul who has never had cause to say, 'Thank God'. The moment may have come on some much-enjoyed holiday; or after a cloud passes—a sorrow or a hurt—or after a reconciliation. Maybe it has arisen at the coming of the beloved into one's life. This human love, which comes to many people, is really an answer by God to that inward longing and searching for some ideal, for a companion, for beauty. It is the search for God that urges men and women each to seek a mate. The search for God is the urge behind all nature, the search for the blooming of the flowers.

This urge brings to people a certain satisfaction, so God comes and speaks in the human heart; but people do not recognize the voice as God, and so they put it down to 'nature'. But every emotion of joy and happiness, every appreciation of beauty, in whatever form, through the senses, is the result of the expression of God through the physical organism.

We all know the joy that comes from the companionship of the friend who is in harmony with us. It comes from the expression, through them and through our own hearts, of an inexpressible something beyond the human mind. The human mind cannot analyse God. Books concerning God are stacked from the floor to the ceiling in libraries, but the mind will never unveil God to people. God is only found at a certain point on the path of experience, when He–She speaks through the heart. When that happens, the man or woman knows and he or she will never again question the love of God. The man who is the son of God, the woman who is the daughter, consciously *never* questions God's love.

Eventually, we all come to this realization: that God is love and everything manifesting on earth is the result of God's love. If every member of the human race could be presented with a copy of his or her karmic balance sheet, and realize the divine plan at work, what a change would follow! And if every member of the human race could be shown with what certainty every act comes 'home to roost', they would think twice before giving pain. We cannot help our past karma, but we can help the karma we make for the future; and therefore, my dear ones, can you not accept the wisdom of endeavouring to discipline yourself to the laws of God? Control yourselves, your thoughts, your speech; be kind and loving. It all boils down to that one thing: be kind and compassionate and never wilfully inflict pain on any living creature through thought, speech, or action. Those who have learnt how much the thoughtlessness or ignorance or wilfulness of another can hurt will not be heedless in the future. The Masters of Wisdom never inflict pain—they are all love, all compassion. But they also recognize the law. They know that every life must eventually become balanced and literally *polarized* to the Divine Light, the Source of all life.

National Karma

There is also national karma, and all nations have their karmic debts to pay. The souls concerned in those karmic debts usually incarnate so as to share in the payment of them. It is an exact law. If souls are responsible or concerned in national karma, those souls will be drawn back to suffer the national karma. The purpose of such an incarnation is that they may learn to respond to the good vibrations, instead of neglecting to respond. Their error is more often due to neglect than not—the sin of omission. It is not possible for you to see the whole plan as yet; we are convinced from what we have seen through the eyes of the spirit that there is perfect justice in the world of spirit. This is not necessarily justice as you understand it, because you see so much of what you call injustice.

The law is exact. Those guilty of causing terrible suffering must by the very act be drawn back again to suffer. Every nation that inflicts cruelty, will in turn suffer. Through suffering, every soul eventually learns the lessons of the law of love.

The Elder Brethren see possibilities; they know that if humanity will take a certain line, certain things will happen within a certain time. They will do all they can to help humanity realize that manifestation of light and truth. But if humanity chooses a side-road—well then, it will take a long time, and the path will be more rugged and difficult.

Humanity has freewill choice. Never forget this; there has often been an opportunity for the settlement of human problems and difficulties by way of brotherhood. Except for lack of confidence in brotherhood, peace would have prevailed. But humanity has freewill choice. The opportunity presents itself every day, to take the higher way (which is always the most difficult way for the materially-minded); but if human kind cannot thus respond—if a man or woman—if a nation, if a world—rejects such opportunity—then it has to learn its lesson by taking the other path, the path of suffering and difficulty. But these two paths lie close together, and can cross again at any moment.

Humanity can respond nobly and spiritually to the voice of God. But it has not yet sufficient confidence in God's voice. Although at the present time it is making a valiant effort, there is not sufficient good thought, or God-thought, in the world. This, brethren, is the reason we have been told by the hierarchies to stress, without ceasing, a message of peace and goodwill, to urge humanity continually forward on the constructive path. This we shall continue to do. Such a way should be yours also, my brothers and sisters: you who, having once seen the light, must keep yourselves positive, knowing that brotherhood and goodwill is the only possible way for humanity, and eventually will be established on earth.

Speeding up Karmic Lessons

You may wonder whether a soul's karma allows it to renounce the world when it wants to? It is true that if the
soul is prepared to pay the price in suffering, its karma
is speeded up and it can crowd into one incarnation the
karma which might take ten incarnations of leisurely
work. Before the soul incarnates, it will be shown the opportunities for progress, perhaps three alternative lives.
Yet one of the purposes of an incarnation is to enable you
to pay certain karmic debts. There is a certain amount
of freewill, but whichever path you choose, in every case
you will be brought into contact with souls whose debts
have to be paid.

If the vision glorious comes and you say, 'I *must* reach
that heavenly goal!', then the Lords of Karma will, in
their own way, bring your sheaf of bills to be met. But
you need a big reserve in your spiritual bank—which is
what very few of us have.

Some of you talk too lightly about karma, not understanding how it governs your life on the physical plane;
and karma, although it may be a little unpleasant, is a
wonderful friend. It is through your karma, if you accept and use it wisely, that you learn your lessons, and so
overcome the barriers holding up your spiritual evolution
and your spiritual freedom. In karma lies opportunity.

Therefore we tell you this gladly. You cannot become
free until you have met your karma tranquilly, looking
always to the Godhead for the wisdom to deal with the

karmic condition. Therefore try and accept your karma, even that of the mental plane.

By this we mean that even by your thoughts you are creating mental karma, which comes back to manifest in a very tangible form. A common fault of humanity is to tempt the spiritual law to breaking point. Your Bible says: *Thou shalt not tempt the Lord thy God.** If you put your hand too near a flame, unless you have the occult strength and knowledge to protect your hand, that flame will burn you, and you will have a painful hand for a long time. Many people take risks like this deliberately, being foolish, so that their bodies in time develop diseases that cause pain and trouble not only to themselves but also to others.

Do not imagine that we lack sympathy for those who are ill. We immediately come to you with healing power, but it does not alter the fact that it was broken law that first caused the suffering.

Karma works very quickly sometimes. You may suffer for foolishness right away. Of course, there are also grave bodily conditions that are the result of actions in previous incarnations. There is sometimes a piling-up of karma. When at last the soul turns to and desires the spiritual life, because it has seen the truth and knows that light is all it wants, it is faced with its accumulated karma and all karmic debts have to be cleared away before it can make real progress. In other words, the garden has to be well-weeded and cleansed, and prepared for the next planting. Flowers cannot grow in a garden ridden with weeds. But

*Matthew 4 : 7, quoting Deuteronomy 6.

although karma can be unpleasant, it brings in its train both wisdom and joy, because in passing through the pain of karma you come out into the light and feel and experience intense joy at the vision of the light, and the emotion of heavenly love which wisdom brings.

The Karma of Disease and Healing

When you treat a patient by spiritual healing, their disease is due to a blockage in the intake of the life-essence. The perfectly-harmonious, well-poised, perfectly-adjusted body and soul is ever open to the inflow of this essence.

The life-essence is to be found, prolifically, generously, in vegetation. It is also found in light and in colour. You will find that certain lights and colours will be used much more in the future in the healing of cancer, for example. Yet all patients do not respond to this form of treatment. Some need this life-essence introduced in a different form. It can be given in the form of certain foods—vitalizing and life-giving foods. Others will absorb it from minerals, for the essence is to be found in the mineral kingdom, and can be abstracted, and administered today in that form. There is no one set cure for all patients. The sufferer is selective, and desires a form particular to his or her stage of evolution. The crux lies in the quality of the consciousness of the patient (about which you do not understand a great deal yet) and that quality of consciousness is something each individual brings over from the past.

It is true to say that certain diseases arise out of past-life experiences. Many so-called incurable diseases are the route the higher part of the individual has chosen to learn a desired lesson through suffering. Remember that these diseases not only affect the patient, but others in contact with him or her. The law of karma reaches very far, and its outworking is in every human life. It is not always in the next incarnation that you meet the results of the immediate past. It may be two or three incarnations ahead. Similarly, you do not touch the same souls in every incarnation—you may contact the same souls several times on the whole journey, but not in every incarnation.

You may wonder why children have to suffer certain diseases. The soul, although but a child in years, may be older than anyone is aware, and that soul may be reaping a harvest. It is a quick way of ridding the soul of inharmony created by breaking a sacred law in a former incarnation. The child meanwhile knows nothing of what is being achieved.

Severe arthritis may come about because the soul of the patient has put it there—in other words, the causes are karmic and the soul is learning much of value, unconsciously, through the limitations and suffering brought by the condition. However, it is possible to treat even severe arthritic conditions by spiritual healing. There is nothing impossible. This is why we never give up any case as hopeless. We dare not say that, because it would be against spiritual law. There is indeed nothing that cannot be helped and cleared away by the Master of life. We know that some cases are very difficult, and it may be that the patient is subconsciously holding up healing for a purpose.

If you are a healer, always give sympathy and love and compassion, whatever the circumstances. Always give the healing, but always surrender your will. The healer must never try to dominate the patient. You give in love, but it rests with the patient whether he or she receives or not. The healer must not blame him or herself if there do not appear to be results physically. *Always* know that true healing, loving healing is never, never wasted, but of great and wonderful service to the patient. Indeed, this applies to all kinds of healing.

We give to the angels the substance, the material out of which our next form of life will take shape. Therefore, you can now see that if a soul is born with a malformation or some inherent disease, there is a deep spiritual reason for this. This gives no cause for anyone to regard that sufferer with contempt or criticism, nor even pity, but only with love, which will awaken the desire to give forth, to assist the sufferer. Do not be disappointed, if you are a healer, when you do not get response from a patient. Realize that you must work in harmony with the cosmic law. Sometimes conditions cannot be healed; do not be disappointed when your efforts seem in vain, but recognize the law of karma at work. Some souls choose the way of physical suffering, and some the way of spiritual and mental suffering.

As we have said, you must not force your healing power. If the patient does not respond within a certain time, there

is a spiritual reason for this. You may continue to give
light and peace and love to the soul, taking little notice
of the obstinacy of the body. Obstructing divine law is a
sin, but giving love and light is a service at all times, and
will never fail in its ultimate purpose. Also, it will add to
your reservoir of good karma.

You may further ask, 'Is it right, in circumstances of
a very painful character, for a doctor to end the life of a
suffering patient? There would seem to be many pros and
cons to this problem. We do not ask you to accept our
answer; but we must answer, because for us it is true. No.
There is no condition in which we could say, 'Yes, end the
life'. God alone can do that. God gives life. God recalls
the soul. From the spiritual aspect, the soul will remain
attached to the body until the time decreed by God for it
to leave. We doubt if any good purpose is served by the
artificial release of the soul from a painful body. By all
means do all you can to alleviate pain, do all you can to
help your brother or sister to endure their lot, but do not
interfere with the divine will. God is omniscient, all-wise.
There are spiritual laws at work throughout life. It is your
duty as a human being to learn about these laws and to
endeavour to live in conformity with divine truth. Pain is
a great teacher. Pain is something that the soul draws to
itself. Courageous endurance of pain brings its blessing,
and you would not wish to be the means of robbing a
loved soul of its reward.

Spiritual healing is an angel's work, and the healer may
look upon it as good karma, an opportunity which has

come in this day of life as a result of kindness you have shown in the past. So it goes on, and the good karma of today will be realized tomorrow or in the years to come, in ever increasing happiness and realization of the divine qualities of the soul.

As the soul learns to overcome its turbulent emotions, to live tranquilly, kindly, lovingly, then as a result the physical body housing the soul should become in due time healthy and indeed perfect. We may touch upon rather a sensitive spot here, because many people suffer more or less from ill-health; the body is rarely the perfect expression of the Christ within. But how many people realize that undisciplined and uncontrolled emotions disturb their bloodstream and glandular system, and that this eventually produces minor, and later perhaps major, ailments? Of course this should not happen. After the Water Initiation* has been passed, the soul can live calmly, patiently and happily day by day: unperturbed and undisturbed, reflecting only the heavenly, the true conditions of the God-life. In course of time, it will be able to express through the body its own perfect wholeness or healthfulness.

Now we know how many of you have suffered, how many of you lack harmony. You have known grief and pain and anguish. We know also, because we have lived

*In INITIATIONS ON THE PATH OF THE SOUL (W.E.P.T., 2007), from which a short section here is taken, White Eagle defines four principal initiations of the life-path, each associated with a particular element. The Water Initiation comes when control over the emotions is achieved, and thus brings peace. See also below, p. 91.

in a physical body, that it seems to be a weak vehicle. We know that it is often tired and weary. We feel your grief. We feel your pain. But, oh, my children, it is only transitory! It will pass. Look up to the Heavenly Father, and to the Divine Mother, and remember that the world of spirit is a very beautiful, harmonious place—and, moreover, that it is all around you.

We will give you a very slight illustration of this. Think of your springtime: the beauties of the spring flowers, and the early leaves of the trees, the green of the grass, the wonderful green of the shooting corn. You look at these beauties of nature, the harmony that abounds; and as you do so, you know inwardly that these are manifestations of the beauty of God's spirit.

The brown earth has to be blessed, has to be tended by the Creative Spirit. The brown earth is the symbol of the Great Mother, the Mother God, Mother Earth, which is the seedbed for all the gifts to human life and animal life and all creation. The brown earth is the seedbed, but without the spirit of the Heavenly Father, without that divine energy and will, nothing could grow. It is the law or command of God to the sunlight and the warmth, to the wind, air and water currents, which causes rain to come and bless the earth. There are times when you get very disgruntled about the rain—but remember that the rain and the air and the sunlight are all part of your life, and part of God's natural law.

If you can get that thought clearly in your mind, whatever you are faced with in life will take the form of an experience planned to bring you in the end the joy of God. And thus we say that God is Mother and Father, divine wisdom, divine love, divine power, ever at work behind all forms and manifestations of life. God's children are sparks of the divine love, come forth from the heart of God so that they may live and grow and develop as children of God; so that they may learn how to express that happiness which God knows and which God has placed as a seed within each breath, or each spark of His–Her life force.

You may accept this, but still ask, 'How can any soul be happy in the consciousness of perfect love while so much pain and cruelty exists at lower levels, and so many apparently innocent people suffer?'. We answer by saying that when men and women have reached the pinnacle of happiness they can see the complete whole; they can see the whole picture, and not isolated conditions of pain and suffering. Some people say even God must suffer, but we would tell you that God is beyond all suffering. When a human soul reaches the level of God-consciousness, it breathes out healing and love, and is living all the time to bring about the evolution of unformed and unperfected beings towards perfection.

If you yourself are suffering, take heart from what we say and try to understand it. Try to absorb this truth and know too that there is always tomorrow, always a fresh opportunity. Endeavour to attune all the higher bodies harmoniously to the spiritual law, and then in time there will be recreated in you a new body of health and perfection, a body of harmony—a heavenly body, if you like.

Innocent Suffering?

On earth, you are consumed by your own emotions, ridden by your idea of suffering. Indeed, when they are encased in a suffering body, people find it very difficult to see beyond their pain. When the soul is freed from its material and physical bondage, when it is freed into the light, it understands that God is wholly love, however confused the physical appearance may be. The God-life is working as an infinite, beneficent power, which is slowly, slowly bringing right and goodness out of wrong and darkness. From the earthly point of view, you see terrible physical suffering. Remember, though, that there is compensation in soul growth.

Why does God permit the innocent to suffer? Because God loves them, that is why!—and again you only see one side of the picture. We do not mind whether we are speaking of an individual or a nation, God sees all sides of the picture. You see suffering; you see perhaps mangled bodies and death through violence. You do not know the soul-experience that is taking place, nor do you know about the awakening, or about the result of this apparent torture and suffering. In any catastrophe there is ultimate mercy. God *is* merciful. God has a way of enfolding the sufferer and leading him or her gently into green pastures and beside still waters. What does a little physical suffering really amount to in comparison with the infinite time before the soul?

If you see disaster, do not wring your hands and say,

'How terrible! How could God permit such a thing?'. Rather, remember how limited is your vision. You do not see what would have happened to those people had they remained in their body in the particular conditions and environment in which they found themselves. You think that a God of love would have left them exactly as they were to pursue their way? Remember that God uses the Lords of Karma (and lesser beings, too, who have it in their power to bring about certain conditions for the good) for the benefit of the man or woman. The wise person immediately says, 'God be praised, for God is all wise and all loving. He–She is without doubt saving the child on earth from some condition, disaster even, which would indeed be unhealthy for his or her soul and much worse than this'. For this reason, always look for the good in any happening.

The innocent are preserved. You do not know the infinite love and mercy of your Creator. You only see things with your worldly vision. You do not recognize the tender loving care that provides for those who suffer, for those who are lonely and afraid. When you see catastrophe—when you see the dead body left behind, or you see the vacant house, you say, 'How terrible!—how shocking death is!'. But you do not know the providence: that which *provides* for those souls whose destiny it is to be released from the body in what may appear to be a terrible manner. We have so often seen the souls of men and women gathered into loving arms in the world of spirit. We know of a loving care which has seen the conditions confronting that soul, and has said, 'This soul has had enough. Come home, my child'. Remember that you cannot know what is on the other side of the material curtain. The souls in question do not realize themselves what is happening. Afterwards, they only know that they are living, moving, breathing in a world that seems identical to their former world. Only with great tenderness and care are they brought to realize that they have left their old body. Until then, they do not know that they have died.

We, in the spirit life, watch these souls continually when they are awakened to this realization, for then they feel such intense joy and thankfulness that the crossing has been made so easily. That is their first reaction. They find that they are in a world as solid and real as the old world, and certainly more beautiful. You see, there is this tender love that watches over humanity. It is not only at the time of death that this love is demonstrated; it is always there and it always has been.

Why then do the innocent suffer for the guilty? They do not; they only appear to. But the law of cause and effect is exact. There is always compensation as a result of suffering. Spiritual laws take no account of sentiment: the law is just, perfect and true. Although the innocent may seem to suffer from your earthly point of view, it is seen from the spiritual viewpoint that a wonderful process of cleansing and healing takes place in the soul as the result of its suffering.

So when you look out upon suffering humanity, particularly upon acute emotional suffering—perhaps a home where husband and wife disagree, or where parents lose their loved children, or when you see what you regard as an innocent and beautiful soul suffering from a terrible disease—will you pause and try to remember our words? Remember them particularly if you yourself are suffering; remember that in some former life you may have inflicted considerable suffering on some of your companions. If so, can you not see that the only way for yours or indeed any soul to awaken to the divine or Christ-consciousness is through its own experiences, its own feelings, even through its emotional, mental and spiritual suffering?

These episodes are the ones you call tests and trials—minor initiations. They lead to a greater initiation, which brings a burst of light or a great illumination of the human spirit.

Nothing Happens by Chance

You cannot possibly comprehend the greatness or the glory of the higher angel beings. Though the great ones seem so far removed, yet they exert a direct influence upon your life, and bring into it the simplest and most trivial event to affect the progress of the human soul. Nothing happens by chance in human life, but we deprecate that condition of mind that accepts without any effort all the squalor and misery that confronts humanity.

This equally applies to the individual. It is all very well to say, 'This suffering is my karma; therefore I must bear it', but it does not help you progress through it. Say rather, 'This is my karma, and I must seek for its meaning, discover what weakness in my soul necessitates this suffering coming into my life'. Seek for knowledge of yourself; seek for wisdom to live life on earth to the fullest and most profitable extent. Yet let the motive behind your seeking be that you may better equip yourself for God's service and to help human suffering.

We want to help you all, dear ones, to see the working out of a wonderful purpose. Although at the moment you may feel sorry and unhappy through the suffering of one you love, yet in that life (maybe not in this incarnation) you will see a wonderful development and regeneration. You must learn that it is not the suffering alone that teaches, but rather your own attitude: your reaction when facing difficulties and sorrows.

Sometimes when you are suffering you cannot discover the reason. If you recognize that you are learning *something* you are paving the way for your own greater understanding. The truth you seek will come in a flash, perhaps some time after the suffering has passed. You are learning the lesson of patience, and also the lesson of love and constancy. When you have to go through difficulties, hold fast to the love of good. Never mind what happens; if you are blinded and unable to see the reasons for suffering, keep the light burning in your breast, saying again and again, 'God is my Father–Mother; God is all good, God will bring me safely through'. Do not cling to material things or even to people—if they go, let them go. If they hurt and disappoint you, that is to teach you. There is only one thing to fear, and that is fear itself. Strive to overcome fear, fear of death, fear of life, fear of loss, fear of suffering. This is the goal—to overcome all fear, and to realize your son–daughtership with the Father–Mother God. You are moving forward rapidly to the great awakening. You will see a reunion of nations and peoples, and a disintegration of the forces of destruction. Look forward, look forward, look forward, not only with hope, but also with conviction, to the coming of the brotherhood of life on earth.

From these many instances, you will gather that the great and advanced soul keeps true to its awareness that God is altogether good. God sends human beings suffering only out of love. Indeed, only through undergoing such experiences can the soul find strength, and only through practice learn to stand unmoved. My brethren, as we talk you can feel that inner poise come, that inner strength which inspires in you the greatest courage. You then know that nothing has power to destroy the eternal love, the living flame within; that nothing matters much so long as you know God or Christ within you.

Is Suffering the Only Way?

The innermost, the impersonal self desires lessons. It does not mind how it gets them ... *it wants the lessons*. This divine urge in each would grow and expand, even by and through pain. The incarnating ego desires to grow, first and foremost, in God-consciousness, and knows it can only grow through knowledge gained by experience. It sounds rather remorseless, perhaps, to say this. But the deep self will cause suffering in the physical body if there is no other way to grow. You will ask, what of the poor soul that is innocent, and does not understand why it is suffering? It is true that the *mind* may be ignorant, but in the soul there is wisdom. If you were able to watch the process of spiritual enlightenment that can take place in the sufferer, you would thank God for the gift of suffering. You would realize it still more could you watch that soul passing onwards to its reward. Remember, there are compensations. Compensation is one of the great laws, one of the five great laws of life.*

You may ask, 'Is the way of suffering necessary?'. We see how people make it necessary because of the complications they bring on themselves. But if you could see the light the Master is holding forth, you would not feel any path to be a path of suffering, but only of light and radiance. It is only another aspect of the cross. The cross is usually represented as being a cross of suffering; but, as we have said, it can always become a cross of triumph. Although the material mind nailed the Divine Man upon the cross, and apparently the body was tortured, nevertheless the spirit was radiant; it shed from the cross radiance, triumph, and light. Humanity rejects the light, and so it remains stretched upon the cross.

Nearly all souls, strangely enough, choose to learn

*See chapter eight, below (p. 105).

through experiencing pain and suffering, but this is not the only way. As each soul treads the path it has to be tested on the physical level, then on the astral or emotional level, and then on the mental level. All your daily experiences are testing you on one or another of these planes, and only you can release yourself from these difficulties. When you are faced with some problem of your own, do not try to excuse yourself. You may excuse everyone else, but never yourself. This will seem a hard doctrine, but we would explain that only *you* can open the door that leads to a higher state of consciousness for you.

Progress will continue to be made through suffering until human kind itself, individually, refuses to suffer. It is possible to progress on the path of joy, but how many souls are great enough for this? If you put your hand in the flame, you learn that it burns. Suffering is the protection by which you are saved. If you did not feel the pain when you put your hand in the fire, you might lose your hand altogether.

This truth you will find repeated again and again in the gospel of St John in such statements as *I am the true vine* and *I and my Father are one.** The soul must realize both whence it comes and whither it goes before it can find any sense in life; otherwise it veers this way and that like a ship without a helmsman. Once the soul recognizes its captain, once that captain takes command, true joy replaces travail and sorrow. This is because the soul can at last understand that in order to create and build itself

*John 15 : 1 and 10 : 30.

anew it may have to undergo certain experiences which will draw to it some of those finer elements from heaven, to be built eternally into the soul body. Sorrow can do this, *and joy also*.

The one great cry of humanity is, 'Why do *I* suffer?'. The answer is, you bring your suffering on yourself, but if you will turn in confidence, trust and faith in the invisible life and the invisible messengers, you will be helped to help yourself. You will not be left alone. You will be companioned. However, no-one can do the work for you. If your guide saved you from yourself, he or she would be robbing you of a valuable soul-experience. Out of it will come a sweet awakening.

Remember, always, the love, the mercy, and the truth of God. Keep your faith in things invisible. Oh, we beg you to do this, because these invisible things are your helpers! The invisible things are the eternal things and are supplying such a part in your life, in your development, your unfoldment, and in your human relationships. Cling with all the strength of the Christ within you to your knowledge of these invisible things of life! We assure you that this is the way.

III
Responding to Karma

The Nature of Advice

WE HAVE SEEN many of our friends passing through bitter human experiences. And we listen; sometimes the question arises, 'Why does not our Guide interfere; why does he or she not save us from making mistakes; why are we allowed to do foolish things and to suffer, when so and so could have prevented us? Had we only known, we should not have done so and so'.

You may think that we, being spirit, are quite remote from the activities and the pains and the fears and the sufferings of our brothers and sisters upon earth, but here you would be very much mistaken. The Brotherhood of the White Light is closely concerned with the evolution, happiness and wellbeing of all human kind. We of the Brotherhood in spirit have passed through many incarnations and have the means of recalling these human experiences when necessary. Therefore we can feel with you; we can understand your frustrations, your limitations and your anxieties and fears. We can understand physical pain and spiritual suffering. We are part of you; we are one of you; we are with you, all of you. But we love you;

therefore we do not remove your problems and difficulties, for this would be neither kind nor good for you. We can only stand by your side and give you strength and love while you slowly learn by trial and error.

As a result of your dealing with these difficulties, if you are moving on the clear path of light and open to the message being brought to you from the spirit, you will receive into your souls a joy that would be lost to you if we were to remove your problems and difficulties. Only you, in companionship with God working in your heart, can experience the heavenly joy of learning those necessary truths. Each time your eyes are opened to the right way of life, each time you are able to touch the secret level of life, the light expands in your heart and soul, and life takes on a new aspect. You see, with eyes both spiritual and physical, a lovelier vista—a more profound beauty than you have seen before. Your heart will sing with praise and thanksgiving to your Creator.

In turn, we ask you not to seek to mould a friend to your chosen mould. It is something that everyone attempts to do at one time or another, very kindly and meaning well. But every soul is a jewel in its own setting, and neither you nor we can never make a pearl a diamond, or an emerald a ruby; all shine in their own radiance. One of the things everyone needs to learn is simply and in the true sense of the phrase, to mind their own business. But what a hard lesson! We all mean so well, too. Never try to run anyone else's life for him or her, and say he should do this, or she should do that or the other.

You may be tempted to want to set another person's life right, to interfere with it in that way. It is different if the person comes to you for opinion and help. If we ourselves are asked, then we give what we have learned, possibly by experience. But that is different from interfering and saying, 'You do this or that wrongly; you shouldn't do it like that, you should do it in *my* way'. By so doing you may rob an individual soul both of self-expression and self-growth.

The Karmic Garden

Someone once asked us this. 'If certain bad vibrations from the past cause an individual suffering today, is it possible for that individual to change the suffering to beauty?'. In reply, we gave the example of a garden. Some people may not trouble to beautify their garden because it is unshapely, but others can and will improve it, by planting bushes and flowers. It is your reaction to events today that will either erase the ugliness or leave it bare.

In their reaction to events, there are those who always bob up like a cork. Although karma seems to have overwhelmed them, they come out smiling. At the very least, do not adopt the attitude of 'having to endure' karma! Your garden may only be a back yard, but it can have lovely flowers and look as sweet and beautiful as many a larger one, if love be there. Is not life beautiful? Is not God good, who gives you the power to beautify?

Next we hear the question, 'If, because of ignorance, people can only grow weeds, what about them?'. Let us remind you that you can only see your companions superficially. It is not possible for one person to have a very clear impression of how another's garden grows. What you call weeds may in reality be flowers.

With regard to those poor souls who are without knowledge, let us say this. There is something of love within *every soul*, no matter who it is; there is God within every human being, like an urge or a light. The individual can respond; and as soon as he or she does, there is that light, that peace. Whatever the path, compensation comes to that person in his or her life, in the inner self. Remember that all of you are at different stages of evolution, and there are those who are living lives on the very outer or materialistic circle, and they cannot possibly remember, they are so far from home. When the soul turns inwards again, towards the Godhead, it begins to open up inner senses that will bring back memories.

If you have chosen a spiritual path, then you too are moving inwards. Therefore your consciousness will gradually quicken and you will pick up fragments of your past. But the person on the outermost ring, in very material conditions, has to deal with those material conditions and no others. Do not imagine these people as lost: there is always that within an individual which will take them far, in accordance with the karma they have chosen. Bear in mind that the law that causes suffering is really at work to bring that individual into joy. It is only through experience and suffering that the soul can be awakened to the consciousness of divine Love.

The law of life is love and service. Humanity has been given dominion over all the lower kingdoms of life; you have the freewill to control the lower kingdoms, but few people have yet learnt to use their power with wisdom and love. If what grows becomes unhealthy, then that part has to be removed. If we return to our image of the garden, things that appear out of place there, such as ivy strangling a tree, or a tree obstructing light and air, have finished their usefulness. The gardener holds the pruning knife and the saw. And so it is in the human garden: that which is outgrown and unwanted has to be pruned away by the hands of karma, and in the form of suffering, the working out of karmic debts. The pruning knife has to be at work so that greater beauty, greater expansion may come.

The same law applies all through life. If we even tell you to be good to flowers and help them in their evolution, you may be puzzled why God allows frost to come and kill the young buds. Why, too, does He–She not send rain when the flowers so badly need it? We remind you that even frost has its place in the clearing away of certain destructive agents in the garden. Even if it nips off buds, good will come the following season. As for the rain being withheld, there are laws that work in exact rhythm and with precision; periods must come when rain is withheld; but eventually the balance rights itself. Humanity cannot have exactly what it wants until all are perfect, and until it knows what to want. We suggest that it is humanity's folly and waywardness that cause certain reactions in the universe, ones that must bring suffering and apparent destruction. It is God's method—or law—to right the equilibrium, or the balance. The wise person does not blame God when things go wrong, does not blame Him–Her for volcanoes and earthquakes. The wise look within, and see how far short they have fallen of God's love.

Overcoming Karma through Prayer, Forgiveness and Wise Use of the Imagination

We repeat that we come to you because we love you. We love all humanity. We have no other purpose. We were once asked why we come back to earth, and our answer is, because it is our special work; we have been given the mission to communicate spiritual truths to our earthly brothers and sisters, whom we love. We come to bring healing, not merely to the body but to the mind and soul. We see so much suffering on earth, and the love our heavenly Father–Mother has given us causes us to long to assuage that suffering. This can only be done by helping our earthly brothers and sisters to understand the reason for their suffering. We seek to show them what suffering can do for them, if they accept and use the experience in the right way.

When we come down, through the mists of the astral, into the greater mists of the earth, we feel and see the suffering caused through fear. We see that the basis of almost all suffering is fear. We see the human mind filled with fear of the unknown, fear of the future. Surely you know by now that whatever tangle you find yourselves in, whatever emotional strain is yours, it will not last forever? It is a passing phase and comes to you as a lesson. All of you here have to learn, to gain knowledge, and it is the actual experience of living with other human beings that enables you to gain wisdom.

This brings us to the next question we think you will ask. 'How can we help humanity to overcome its fear of war, and of even worse things?'. On your earth, a great mountain of fear seems to build up. Because people are so fearful, they are urged to think out more and more terrible weapons to protect themselves. While these thoughts prevail, there is a build-up of a great enemy—but it is not the enemy that people think. An invisible foe is far worse than one whom you know and can see.

There is really nothing for the spirit of man and woman to fear. If you are reaching out your hand towards God, if you are living with love in your heart, then nothing, nothing can touch you. If you concentrate only upon physical things, upon pain and suffering, you will think, 'How terrible!'. So often, you feel tortured because you believe that you can do nothing. Your heart is wrung and you lose all your poise and all faith because of the suffering that you witness. O my children, remember that there is a loving protective power; and the child of God has to learn to trust that power of love. The mother knows her child and the Divine Mother can apply an antidote to every type of suffering.

In your learning, imagination plays a very important part; it is a gift that must be striven for and cultivated. At the same time, imagination of the negative kind can bring to people much more suffering than is necessary. Although a good imagination can be your friend and helper, a negative imagination can be your foe.

We do not want to make you disregardful of suffering. To help you, we should like to say this: that the physical body is so wonderfully constructed, and the power of love is so great, that there is a mercy that dims even the most terrible suffering. Remember always that God is merciful as well as just, and as you probe the meaning of suffering you will recognize a merciful and loving power that succours and saves.

In the Apocryphal Gospels, you will read the testimony of St John to the effect that Jesus came to him, while his body was at that time on the cross and apparently suffering terrible agony. Jesus the Christ was not suffering that agony, he was beyond; he was absent from his body. His spirit was with his disciples. Did he not say to them once, '*The prince of this world cometh and hath nothing in me*'?*

When the spirit rises above the body, the soul does not suffer. Do not allow this to make you indifferent to pain, for anyone who suffers needs all your love and your care; but we point out to you that the spirit can rise out of suffering, as Christ demonstrated.

We all like to cling to 'I', forgetting that the real and the true 'I' is always a part, a unit in the Universal—or,

*John 14 : 30.

if you like the word better, the Christ light. So many dread the thought of absorption into the Universal, but we must remind you that it is separation from this Christ light that causes human suffering. As we tried to explain when we spoke of joy and sorrow being one, only when the soul is separated from its true self do joy and sorrow become separate too, and operate in the life as teachers and guides. Thus they lead the soul back again to God.

The beloved Lord, Jesus the Christ, gave humanity the perfect prayer in simple language. *Our Father*, he said— we think we would add Mother—Our Father–Mother, *Who art in heaven, hallowed be Thy Name. Thy kingdom*—of spirit—*come. Thy will be done, on earth as it is in heaven. Give us this day our daily bread.* Thou knowest our need. Thou wilt give us all the needs of our bodies and of our souls. And *forgive us our trespasses*, our debts. Forgive us as we forgive.

The very act or the emotion of forgiveness in your heart towards your brother or sister instantly brings to you a blessing and forgiveness for all that you may have done. If you feel forgiveness towards those who have apparently wronged you, you yourself are immediately forgiven. Or as our brethren in the East might say, your karma is settled immediately.

The truest and finest prayer is the one in which you ask nothing for yourself, only that you may know the love and the power and the wisdom of God. It is a yearning of the soul to be united with God. When a soul can pray like this, nothing on earth matters. It no longer cries out for this or that particular thing to happen, it does not seek its own gratification on any plane of life; it only seeks union with its Creator. In this way every prayer is answered perfectly.

The Will to Think Aright

Another important lesson which all have to learn is the power of thought. You are living an outer life in a physical world. But side by side with this outer life there is an inner life. This inner life is a world of thought; and thought promotes action. Now, as you think, so you become—you are creating your inner world. From that inner world come both your speech and your action.

For example, you bring your suffering upon yourselves. Now you will ask, 'How can we bring this upon ourselves when, for instance, we are broken-hearted through the loss of a loved one?'. No, you did not bring the bereavement, but you bring your suffering because you do not yet understand what death really is. For if you are able to penetrate the mists of earth, you will know that your loved one is not dead, nor is he or she gone from you.

In spirit there is no separation. Contact with your loved one is always waiting for you through the power of thought, through the power of meditation. You have to develop within yourself a consciousness of the eternity of life. You have to make yourself so love God that you know that God is love and has all love for you, as you have love for God. You have to know that in God's consciousness there is no death. Your loved one is living in that love, and in your spirit. Your loved one is with you.

When we draw near to the earth, we see confused thought-forces; we see our brothers and sisters on earth suffering physical pain, discomfort, and weariness of the body. We desire to give them healing balm, but this is difficult. There is a way which is open to us; but if people only understood a little more of the power of thought, they could themselves find perfect health. Moreover, healing rays could be poured through them to alleviate the sufferings of many. The habit of your thought has to be trained, directed, into healthier channels. A great many thought-forms are distinctly unhealthy. When you allow yourself to send forth such thought-vibrations, you open yourself to, and even welcome in, forms created by the unhealthy thought of others around you. If you are in the habit of thinking negatively, or neglecting the positive or *good* thoughts, you are subject to attack.

Some people are terribly frightened of germs. You fear infection, and your medical colleagues, from their very insistence on such dangers, increase this fear. Although we would not increase fear, we must say that they are not altogether wrong. Until the spirit takes command, the thought-patterns you generate come from aimless mental wandering. They are the result of rushing hither and thither mentally, without discipline or control. It is then that germs can become very active. So the danger we would most describe for you is the infection of *thought*-forces. If a person is sensitive but negative, and allows the uncontrolled patterns of thinking we have described, then he or she is receptive to the forces of the astral plane, and likely to allow a germ to take hold. Think of it like a thought-force, which will trouble the etheric body, and eventually find its way into the bloodstream. There follows depletion, and then all the physical troubles that occur.

What thoughts habitually dwell in your mind? Are you mentally disturbed and overwrought? If so, you are subject to astral force. Can such disorders be cured by the right thought? Yes ... amazingly so! Square your body! Hold it *on the square*, upright. Think positive thoughts; refuse to be driven hither and thither by the thoughts or words of others. Keep steadily on your path. You think this is easy to say? Yes—but following our advice will bring to you healing vibrations.

If you suffer physically, do not think of your suffering at all! Does that sound harsh? Yes, we believe so, but remember this. If you are in pain, and the thought comes, 'I suffer; I do feel bad!', then all the negative powers around are multiplying the thought of pain. For this reason, we would say that there is much truth in the wise practice of Christian Science. We do not by this mean that the wisest methods are always followed, but that the *science* is true and real. The thought of good, of God, enveloping an individual, enfolds him or her in the light of Christ. Those able to put this science into practice wisely, truly, will reap wonderful blessings, not only for themselves—for you cannot think only unto yourself—but for others also.

Earth people imagine their thoughts to be their own. Never did they make a greater mistake, for thought goes forth and affects the whole. No-one can *be* good and *think* good without assisting the growth of good throughout the human family. So also with unkind, negative, unlovely thoughts: they pass from one person to another. You have a great responsibility! Radiate thoughts of love, however much you are tempted by the germs of unkindness to radiate criticism.

Thoughts create definite waves in the ether. The thought, if it is about another person, travels directly to that individual, and will take form, hovering in his or her vicinity, and waiting until he or she is off-guard. If the receiver has a mind full of useful and helpful thought, it is unlikely that the intruding thought will penetrate until the mind is not so occupied, when it jumps in. If the recipient knows enough, he or she will immediately push a negative thought out, or transmute it into a good and positive one. If the thought is good, then he or she will be stimulated. You are all continually receiving the thoughts of others, particularly on the astral and mental planes, for it is on these planes that the thought-forces work.

How can a student attain balance while working in a condition of chaos and noise? There are two distinct aspects of life. There is the outer, with its noise and turmoil; and there is the inner, which nothing can disturb. In the quiet countryside, a person's heart may be as a raging storm; in the heart of the metropolis, peace can dwell deep within. So actually cultivate calmness and poise within, and in time these qualities will become habitual. Nothing can disturb a settled inner peace, unless you allow yourself to be swamped by the outer world. You can control the door between outer and inner, if you *think* on the right lines.

Balance and poise are of vital importance. The earth life interpenetrates the higher planes; once physically poised, you automatically and naturally grow in steadiness and poise on the higher planes. It is possible to retain balance and poise right through working hours full of noise and interruption. A student when meditating should bring through into earthly life the strength gained during that meditation. It is no use being in the clouds; there must be real work upon the astral, mental and physical vehicles during meditation.

Tomorrow, for all we say, you will rise, and in all probability find yourself slipping back in your efforts. External things may trouble you. Perhaps you will get a trying letter. Do not send to its writer angry thoughts. Instead think, 'Poor brother, sister—I am sorry'. This will become easy for you if you will take hold of yourself, pull yourself up and *think rightly*. Think rightly, and you will be amazed at the change, at the growing peace of mind that comes. Life will become joyous, and you will be happy.

IV
The Law of Opportunity

The Mercy of God

THE LAW of cause and effect—or karma—walks hand in hand with the law of opportunity. Opportunity comes to all men and all women, every day, for good, for progress, for service, for opening the innermost being a little more to divine light and divine happiness. It is the law of karma that causes this law of opportunity to operate. Whenever you meet sorrows and problems, or when you find joys and solutions, remember that the result of your karma is bringing an opportunity to acquire wisdom and thus step forward on the path. Each time a cause is sown (like a seed) in the individual, or in the national or international life, there is bound to be a following effect, which can be either happy or unhappy. In either case it will bring fresh opportunity.

The opportunity you have is the opportunity to make the best of all circumstances and conditions—or the opportunity for the expression of the highest and the best in you. So as well as the law of cause and effect—which is strict, just, perfect and true—there is also this law, which is one of divine mercy. A wise child looks up to God. God is merciful to that child, but He–She does not say, 'You will not have to work or suffer. You will not have to work out your karma'. Instead, God says, 'My child, my love is with you and will help you'. Divine love is divine mercy. God can thus heal all wounds, helping His–Her children to go through their self-created karma. The mercy of God is also related to the mercy in human beings. In the degree individual soul shows mercy, so God releases mercy too.

We should like to emphasize this point—the mercy of God. All is very well; there are exact laws of spiritual evolution. It may seem sometimes that the powers that be can be very stern and unrelenting. The truth is that God is always merciful and kind. Even though suffering has been brought on by the sufferer's own wilfulness, nevertheless God in His–Her mercy sends help and gives the sufferer opportunity (as we have told you before) to transmute his or her karma, or else to lift himself, herself, up out of it. When this happens, it is very wonderful. You remember Jesus saying there is greater rejoicing in heaven over one that was lost and is now found, than over the ninety and nine who continue safe in the fold?* Remember the great mercy that is shown to delinquents by divine Love, a power that sends aid to the erring one and helps that soul when it truly repents. This may sound rather to savour of the old orthodoxy, but you see there is profound truth in all religions, whatever they are and however far they may seem to have strayed from their original path. God does not turn a deaf ear to the soul who is truly—not

*Matthew 18 : 12–13.

just superficially—but deeply, humbly repentant, who is aware of the 'sin' committed and cries to Father–Mother God, 'Help me! God forgive me!'.

We are speaking about spiritual law and of those powerful forces or intelligences that govern the whole of the spiritual life and evolution of human kind. As we have said, the power of God is merciful and helpers are directed to each lost soul—when it is ready. A vast organization, just, perfect and true, exists in the higher world. Call it what you will; call it the Great Brother–Sisterhood if you like. It consists not only of souls who have evolved along the path of humanity, but also beings that have evolved along the angelic path. These latter, like angels of light, watch over even the simplest and the humblest soul. So when the earnest cry is sent forth, 'Forgive me, God!' (who has not heard that spontaneous cry from the lips of suffering souls?), God does not turn a deaf ear. You remember that Jesus the Christ went down among the tortured souls to alleviate their suffering, to raise them? This means that the second aspect of the Logos, the Son, sends to those poor souls in distress the opportunity to rise. What an example and demonstration to human kind, for men and women are not merciful to their brothers and sisters to the extent that God is merciful!

The Balance of Opportunity

Let us regard difficult karma more as *opportunity* for the soul to learn or make further progress. Life brings many opportunities, presented to the soul by the angels of karma. Sometimes these are not made into useful lessons by the soul, and therefore he or she goes through a period of suffering, and seems not very much better for the experience. But that same opportunity will crop up again and again. There is also opportunity for progress through wise use of good karma in the horoscope. The soul by its previous conduct has brought about the necessity for certain experiences or lessons in incarnation. The planetary angels watch over the events or the experiences through which that soul is passing, not interfering because they know that an exact and precise law is at work. There is ever a lack of emotion in angels. Angels do not suffer from emotional disturbance; they are unmoved by suffering. Instead, they see beyond human suffering and all their work is planned in accordance with the perfect law of evolution.

We have said that suffering gives the soul the opportunity to learn the lesson peculiar to that suffering, and the opportunity to assimilate spiritual truth. Nevertheless, we are sorry when we see you sit down in a heap and declare, 'Well, having brought this thing upon myself, there is nothing except to put up with it. What else can I do?'. Beloved brother or sister: if you think thus, you are missing the crux of the whole matter. Do not accept suffering, limitation, hardship, difficulty as something ordained, or inexorable in their continuation; for this other law, opportunity, operates side by side with that of cause and effect. Thus, though you may and probably have incurred debts in the past, these debts are not inescapable. Liabilities can be outweighed by credits, remember. Opportunities come your way. They bring you the chance to do a kindness, to give service to others, or to attempt something for yourself that calls for high courage and steadfastness. By seizing such opportunities, far more rapid spiritual progress can be made than by resigned acceptance of discomfort.

We know that certain schools of thought insist that the debts of bad karma are inescapable. This is not our view: in this life in which you now find yourselves, you should bring forth into action the knowledge that you have absorbed. We note how often opportunities to be helpful to others or progress for yourselves are rejected (these laws apply with the same certainty to nations as they do to individuals). Nevertheless, they will eventually be taken, and men and women will find that they can learn through joy and achievement, and with greater speed and certainty than by the suffering they once thought inescapable. So do not complacently accept suffering: rather, look about you for opportunities for transmuting suffering into achievement.

People may regret the lack of opportunity in this incarnation to do this or that thing. For instance, some regret their lack of mental training and intellectual attainment (what the world calls 'education'); and yet these same have within them the qualities of aspiration and intuition. To them, we say 'Regret nothing, beloved; if the powers that be, the great Lords of Karma, had seen fit to place you in conditions of life which would have brought intellectual attainments and a comprehensive education, you would have been so placed. There are many on earth at present who in past lives have stored within them all that education and intellect could bestow. During this incarnation, their development lies along the love–wisdom, or intuitional, path. It leaves the physical brain unclouded, in order that the wisdom stored within the soul shall register, or be reflected, upon the outer consciousness.

Regret nothing. Accept the conditions of life as they present themselves with a thankful heart, knowing them as necessary for you at the present time. Every opportunity that presents itself in this incarnation is the result of your past efforts. You have earned your opportunities for spiritual development and acquisition of spiritual knowledge and wisdom. You will earn in this incarnation fresh opportunities, which will present themselves in your next.

Here we should like to encourage some of you who feel that your efforts have been to no avail. There is so much you want to do, but you are limited, you are unable to progress. Nevertheless, you are building into your soul today those vibrations that will create for you in your next incarnation much better and easier conditions, ones in which you are able to work and serve human kind. This is why we say so often that no effort is wasted. Every effort is leading you somewhere, even though you do not see the result in this incarnation.

Brethren, when you can realize this, your earthly life does not seem so worthless after all. Earthly life falls into its true perspective; you begin to realize that every sorrow, every limitation, every moment of self-denial, even the thraldom of fear which grips you sometimes, are all intended to teach or prepare your soul for an illumination which is bound to come. Therefore those of you who feel that life is particularly troubled, and that you live in sorrow, do not be sad or resentful. These things are opportunities, which the great God has brought. Examine your opportunities and you will find beauty and mercy in the plan. In life, God lays before you opportunities to learn, to become prepared for initiation; too often, out of laziness and lethargy the chance is pushed on one side. People prefer to go along with their heads down, looking at the mud, and so do not see the angel, God's messenger, who is holding a golden crown of jewels before them.

The soul receives continual opportunity to attain divine illumination. During its every incarnation, lessons are presented—call them tests, if you like—which are actually opportunities for progress and initiation. Tests come to you in almost every detail of life. By these you can gauge the reaction of your emotions to human events, the reaction of your minds to life in general, and the reaction of your hearts in the love you feel towards other beings. Finally, through the tests you will recognize how you are bringing the divine attributes right through your physical nature, and your ability to direct and control your life by calling upon the supreme love, power, wisdom and intelligence of the Most High—your Creator.

Your life is charged with opportunities to grow in wisdom, love and divine power. Beloved, put your hand into the hand of God … and He–She will lead you step by step. Make the effort to walk God's way and you will pass your tests and initiations (a word which means expansion of consciousness) until you become as one of the twenty-four elders around the throne.* Then as never before you will know the significance of the word 'humility'. Once you know humility you will strip yourself of your crown of light—which means that you will know that you are as nothing, for you move and have all your being in God. In God's life alone you can live and know supreme happiness beyond all earthly understanding.

This is the answer to the many who are so deeply troubled by life's contradictions. They ask, 'Why? Why? Why? What have I done, that this trouble should come to me?'. All we can reply is that you have either refrained from or needlessly neglected some opportunity to serve or to express kindness to your earthly companions. This is why the suffering came. You will go on to ask, 'What is the good of it all?', perhaps protesting that because you cannot remember what happened so long ago, the suffering fails in its object. To which we answer that if your physical brain cannot remember, your deeper consciousness knows well that it has earned the experience.

Be thankful, therefore, and accept all your opportunities disguised as so-called karma. Suppose a person goes through a particularly dark patch of trouble or sickness, or suffers a great loss, undergoes some kind of limitation or hardship, or meets misunderstanding or injustice. All

*For the reference, see Revelation 4 : 10.

these experiences, when seen in their right perspective—with understanding that they are lessons through which your master is trying to make you see and understand life more perfectly—all these will be recognized as tests. Furthermore, you will always find, however trifling a test may seem, that when it is passed, there has come a change. 'I shall never be the same again', you say. That is true, never the same, but always better, let us hope; for in a minor way an expansion of consciousness or understanding of human nature and human experience has been the result.

V
Freewill

Is there Choice?

ALL OF YOU like to believe that you possess freewill and can choose your own path. On the other hand, life most certainly demonstrates that human kind is not its own master, but is governed by inexorable law. It is often said that 'what is to be will be'. We ourselves often state that God holds the plan. But if you believe that God holds the plan, there also comes the temptation perhaps to 'let go' of your own commitment to your destiny. You may, for instance, think that if each individual life is already plotted and arranged, you are so caught in a wheel of fate that it does not matter what you strive for, or what you fail to accomplish.

Again, occult sciences may declare human destiny to be written in the stars, or on the lines of the hand. A clairvoyant is able accurately to predict certain events, sometimes trivial, sometimes important, which he or she can see impressed on the ether. Is it, then, that you are all mere puppets, spinning on a wheel of fate? And if this is so, can we believe that there also exists a divine love and justice at work in human life?

Against this, schools of religious thought teach that humanity has freewill and can shape its own destiny. *They are also right.* So how are we to harmonize two opposed or at least seemingly contradictory statements? To understand destiny and freewill, you must first understand the law of cause and effect and recognize that your actions or reactions today shape tomorrow's destiny, as past actions and reactions have shaped today's.

The measure of freewill you have is expressed by your aspiration, your desire to advance; your desire to be more Godlike; or on the other hand by your indifference to God and your indulgence in self. So, if you choose to go towards God you are creating good karma, better conditions for yourself and the world. But if you are indifferent to the universal Being and decide to indulge your lower self, you will presently suffer much pain. In other words, your birthright of freewill is really the power to choose between what people crudely think of as good and evil. There is a small radius in which the human soul vibrates, or can swing, and within this radius you can choose. The choice is given to you in order for you to gain experience. Outside that radius, you do not have power.

We assure you, too, human kind can never destroy God's world. Sometimes, we admit, humanity has a pretty good try—and destroys as far as it humanly can. The ugliness, the sordidness, of the conditions in which so many live is not God's will, my children: rather the unkindness of one human being to another creates this. You have freewill only within the orbit of the divine Will;

so when humanity has filled the cup of misery and suffering until no more can be contained in it, the powers that be step forward. There is a power holding life and all the planets on their courses, and humanity cannot shake this infinite and eternal power. The great Being, the Divine Intelligence, holds all life in love, in the heart.

The more we ourselves learn of spiritual law, the less positive we are about the extent of human freewill. We mean that you are placed in certain conditions in physical life, with opportunities arising all through your lives— circumstances that will give you opportunity to serve the Great Law. It may look as though you have made your own choice in terms of the path you walk, but the real choice lies in your reaction to the conditions that must come. Therefore, walk humbly on your path, cultivating above all love to those who walk alongside you, and recognize behind all the Divine guidance.

What a controversial subject this is! *Humanity has freewill, but its freewill is the will of God.* Why then strive at all? Why not go as flotsam on the tide?—only because the divinity within is always in touch with the Great White Light, the central power. Although it appears accidental when certain things happen, and chance contacts seem to be made, we can assure you that the divinity within directs life.

For example, when a serious accident is averted, the individual thus protected might say, 'What a piece of luck!'. Another might say, 'It must have been my spirit guide who stopped me doing that'. Maybe it was, but maybe your guide is as a shining Star above, your direct link with the Divine Mind. So you are guided and directed by this wonderful law. Therefore never think with regret that you could have averted or changed things in your life. The great Architect of the universe holds the plan; all is working together for good. The divine purpose declares that as you, my child, react, so may you receive greater strength, greater light, greater truth. In that sense you have freewill. Your reaction to outer circumstances is the thing that matters. Try to get above the conditions that sometimes threaten you with so much unhappiness. Do not be pulled hither and thither like a piece of straw in the wind. Try to realize the divine power behind all, within you, drawing you upward through every bitter and every joyful experience, upward into the divine light.

Men and women have to have a choice, always; they have to learn discretion; they have to learn how to discern truth. This you are all doing; and when you come up against certain conditions—and perhaps other groups who may appear to you to be wrong—do remember that you are brought in contact with what appears to you to be wrong or right in order to learn the lesson of discrimination and discernment. You have to learn to recognize the true ring, the ring of truth in the world.

On the spiritual path, much is expected in the way of self-discipline. The ancient mystery schools always laid before the neophyte the simple rules of their brother–sisterhood, which all had to learn; and any who could not pass their test left the temple. No-one is bound to the spiritual path; it is a difficult path, but only a person's own freewill holds him or her to it. That person is at liberty to return to the world and live a worldly life. But the indwelling spirit, because of its past experience and the wisdom it has gained in previous incarnations, knows that if you choose the spiritual path it must follow the light. It is your joy and consolation in life, and brings radiant health to your body. It also brings with it soul-gifts enabling you to penetrate the enveloping mists, the confusion and the darkness of the physical life.

Bound, yet Free!

So, human kind has a certain freedom; but that freewill operates only within a small orbit, and the limitation is usually time. When a soul reincarnates, it returns with a desire to work out its karma, or to pay for the debts it incurred in a previous life. The birth of the soul into the physical body is timed to afford it the best opportunities to do this. The angels of the planets—the lords of karma if you like—are watching that child, and they know that it should be given opportunities for certain experiences. Therefore the angels give all possible help. The planets that you sometimes call 'malevolent' bring certain restrictions and limitations to the soul. Nevertheless, their purpose is good, and they enable it to learn lessons, which the soul (or nation, or even the whole world) should learn. Nations, and humanity as a whole, have certain karmic conditions to work off. Humanity is not confined to one path only—it has a choice, much as before birth you are offered a choice of lives. Peoples are destined to make certain progress, although they have a choice of the path that will achieve it. Your fundamental lessons are fixed, and therefore you will be born under the signs giving you your greatest opportunity to learn them; but you may choose, within limits, which way you will go to learn those lessons.

Before humanity makes its decision, an elder Brother or Sister may prophesy that a nation is bound to go through a certain experience. Yet the one who is enlightened knows that the particular path is the nation's freewill choice, as with the individual. There may be several ways of working out a particular piece of karma, or learning a lesson, and most people choose that of suffering, because they kick against it all the way. Thus more suffering comes to humanity than need be. This measure of freewill is God's gift to humanity. People can choose, within limits, what they will do, but they will learn their lessons ultimately. Whether they learn them as quickly as they might is their own choice. As the God-consciousness grows within them, they become wiser, and so escape much suffering. For this reason they generally do not bring upon themselves so much suffering when they are wiser and older, as they do when they are young.

At certain stages of development, souls do not have so much choice about how they will reincarnate. In the case of young souls, at the beginning of their cycle of life, the choice is not so much given to the individual as to the group soul. The group soul will direct the good of the group. Often, the younger souls find themselves in conditions that are particularly difficult at the beginning. That is not saying that all living in such conditions are young souls. There may be those who have *chosen* that condition.

Thus your measure of freewill is infinitely smaller than you imagine. Over the major events in life people have at present no control. But people can control the future; that is to say, they can mould in this day of life what will come to them in a future incarnation. In the present life, matters come up from the past, even though people like to feel that they have freewill! It is not a question of God interfering; the human race has presented itself with certain events. The reaction of men and women to these will create their tomorrow.

Humanity's freewill, we said earlier, is the will of God. So you might ask whether, if a person choose to commit a crime, it is right or just that he or she should be punished? When we speak of the will of God, we are referring also to the divine law directing human life, so that the soul through experience may absorb illumination: in other words, that the soul may grow. Now the will of God, while directing human action, which sometimes may appear evil, is really guiding that soul through a needed experience. The corresponding punishment is also experience. Consider the process of so-called good and evil as growth for each human soul. If the will urges the soul to crime, then crime is a path of experience for that soul. Remember that the law of karma is behind all these things, and sin and suffering may prove to be ultimate purification and growth. All that the law of life is concerned with is growth.

This is expressed in every form of life—growth, *growth!* When you remember these things, then you withdraw all condemnation, all judgment and you begin to love. *Judge not, that ye be not judged.** Never condemn, never criticize!

Finally, the guardian angel helps the soul—when it desires to be helped—by guiding and strengthening it, but it lies with the individual to accept or reject such help. Every human being is his or her own saviour. He or she has the freewill to create exactly what he or she is in himself or herself. And when that individual comes to the spirit world, then all the beauty, the love, the selflessness and the devotion which he or she has poured out on others in this life, the individual finds reproduced around him- or herself in the new life. Many souls awakening after death on the astral plane say, 'All I can see is God. God in the flowers, God in the trees, God in form, God in the landscape, God in everything!'. Yes; and we hear, too, 'I am in God and God is in me. We are inseparable'. And yet souls retain their individuality. All the beauty of God flows through them, and the more Godlike they are, the more beautiful their surroundings and their appearance. In every way they are channels of God. This is where the soul-choice lies.

Action and Reaction

Your poets tell you apparently contradictory things. You are the 'master of your soul', says one, but another tells you that there is 'a divinity which shapes your ends'.

*Matthew 7 : 1.

If you are captain, or master, how can there also be a destiny to shape your life? Of course, it is natural to feel that you *are* the captain, and the teaching coming from the spiritual planes of being—no matter through what channel—also directs one to take command. It directs the ego, the God-urge, to take control and to captain one's life. But if the future is already planned and ordained, what is the use of making any effort to alter it?

We would remind you, today creates tomorrow. Your destiny lies in your own hands. Glancing back over yesterday, you may see that certain vibrations of your life were set up as a result of actions. We know that there is a law—one of the five fundamental laws of life—the law of cause and effect. Each human being continually casts a foreshadowing of his or her future, a reflection forward into the days to come. This is why those with vision can most surely foretell the future.

The vibrations to which we refer reflect 'pictures' on the ether. Your moving pictures provide a mechanical, material, demonstration of the power of the unseen, as do also your ordinary photographs. Your life today is like your little camera that takes pictures. So do you also set up on the screen of the ether incidents that are likely to happen? The vibration of yesterday on the ether is reflected today, the vibrations of today will be reflected in the future life—not necessarily in the spirit life, but in incarnate life. And so yesterday, today, and tomorrow are all one.

Seeds were sown in your previous lives; vibrations were sent forth into the ether. We cannot go into all the marvellous details which result, but the vibrations penetrate the astral and the spiritual worlds, and set in motion certain forces which are drawn again to the sender. As a result, the soul is led into the conditions of life that have been created. We can couple this with the influences of the planets. Many think it absurd to say that the planets influence human life; but we can assure you that there is nothing useless in the universe; it is full of divine correspondences. Planetary forces are drawn to the central point of the being; and there follows a rebirth of that being. The seed is reborn in the very soil that will best help it to grow and to send out finer vibrations for the future.

Try to take hold of this thought: that the entire universe is working towards ultimate perfection, to ultimate Godliness. Always keep it as your guiding star. Allow it to guide your life, because *today is eternity*. Those vibrations you set in motion today are your future. Take a fast hold of this ideal of truth and beauty and loveliness throughout life, and you are creating a fair tomorrow. What you endure today is the vibration of yesterday. So today is eternity, since it reflects yesterday and creates tomorrow.

Life, we assure you, is vibration. It is because the vibrations set in motion in the past reverberate through the ether, and come to settle (if we may use that expression) today, in your life, that we can tell you that yours is the power to create the future. This is this sense in which you are the captain of your ship, the master of your soul.

The physical bodies into which souls are born, the etheric bodies which make the bridge between the world of matter and the world of spirit, the mental bodies by which the individual understands the laws of life and gains experience of the earth life: all these vehicles are the result of the past. Today you are creating or building the atoms into your soul that will be used to form future vehicles for yourself, through which you will manifest, if not on the planet earth, possibly on another planet of this earth's system.* Therefore upon you rests the choice. You may build into your soul disease-atoms, through neglect and wilfulness, and particularly through neglecting opportunities to learn of the inner wisdom. You may build wonderful opportunities. You may limit yourself by your own freewill, and the lords of karma can only rebuild bodies with the material that you offer them.

You give the angels the substance, the material out of which your next form of life will take shape. It is your *reaction* which creates brightness or otherwise for the future. The happenings in your life should be regarded as tools placed in your hand to fashion and shape the material of your soul. Think of the soul as the rough stone, the rough ashlar, and events as chisels and hammers with which to shape the soul into the perfect square. Thus cut, it fits its appointed place in the spiritual temple you create, which is the 'oversoul' or higher consciousness. While on earth, your soul is the rough ashlar, the earthly stone, being made ready for its heavenly destiny.

*White Eagle may here be referring to the etheric counterpart of the planet, not the physical part we see.

VI

When Freewill becomes God's Will

The Call to Initiation

CERTAIN experiences in life are not the result of cause and effect, but ones that the soul is actually called upon to undergo. They are the ones we will call initiations. Preparation of the soul for initiation is sometimes unpalatable; it may take the form of painful bereavement, of having to surrender a loved one; or of a big change in life which the soul shrinks from, simply because it prefers to cling to a familiar condition and objects to going forward into the unknown. A struggle with itself follows, and causes pain and suffering. If the soul once understands and recognizes that it is faced with an initiation, saying, 'Not my will, O God, but Thy will be done', then that is a true act of surrender (not sacrifice, for sacrifice is something different). It is an act in accordance with the law of love. Jesus prayed, '*Father, if thou be willing, remove this cup from me*'. When he knew that such a removal was not the will of God, he said, '*Nevertheless not my will, but Thine, be done*'.* Thereafter he went quietly forward to meet what was appointed for him.

There is no soul that does not at some time have to

*Both quotations are to be found in Luke 22 : 42.

face initiation and either yield itself, or refuse to yield, to the will of God. Remember, though, that to make no effort to help yourself or to relieve pain and suffering in others is no act of surrender to the will of God. By accepting ills as inevitable you are not accepting God's will, because God did not intend humanity to suffer. Rather, God created a beautiful world and created not one but every individual as 'His only-begotten Son' to enjoy the beauties of life. For the Son is not only Christ, but the spirit of Christ which is born in humanity.

The candidate who treads the path leading to the portals of initiation must be prepared to welcome the cross of renunciation, or crucifixion. The soul growing strong, the soul in whom the flame begins to burn brightly, will face all renunciation philosophically, tranquilly, joyously. For that wise soul will know that that which is lost has served its purpose, and its usefulness; and that something better now awaits it. Whether that thing will come on the spiritual or the material plane, it does not know; but certainly something better awaits it. You must learn to face the cross with tranquillity, knowing that out of the ashes of the past is born a new life.

In your heart, every one of you knows this to be true. You have actually experienced it. Pain and suffering so often come because a soul will cling to a condition that obviously must be withdrawn. But having learnt this lesson, having been willing to renounce, you receive fresh opportunities and greater blessings. We might even say that the Master's hand is laid upon the head of the pupil with, 'Well done, little brother…' or 'Well done, little sister'.

All life's deeper experiences, then, are in their way initiations. But there are both major and minor initiations. Indeed, the ancients taught that there are three principal initiations for every soul to go through. There is initiation on the physical plane, initiation on the soul plane, and initiation on the spiritual plane of life. There are also four other major initiations, not quite so important as these three. Try to think of the three initiations as a triangle forming the side of the pyramid that is your life. A pyramid being four-sided, the base of the pyramid is a square, and this is represented by the four other initiations or lessons which the soul must learn. These four lessons are those of Earth, Air, Fire and Water. The whole pyramid is the complete human being, perfected over many lives.*

Let us now describe things in more detail. Before it incarnates, the soul is offered three possible paths. One might not be so difficult, so that a little karma would be paid off; and the next a little more difficult, and the third perhaps so difficult that practically all remaining karma would be paid off. The choice to take the greatest, the middle, or the least degree, is the soul's. It might choose to hurry, or to take things at a leisurely pace. Therefore if in your life what feels to be a big piece of karma comes along, say to yourself, 'I myself chose that; I am going to get on with it!'. There is really no forcing, because the soul has its choice. It is not forced into reincarnation.

*The four initiations of Earth, Air, Fire and Water are dealt with in White Eagle's book INITIATIONS ON THE PATH OF THE SOUL. See above, p. 43.

Some say, 'Nothing will induce me to come back!'. Well, you won't come back in this frame of mind; but later, when you see something very lovely, and learn that it will not be yours until you go back to earth, eventually you will say, 'Yes; I must have that beautiful thing'. The higher self sees; the lower self kicks very hard and rebels. But the higher self is inspiring and urging it forward all the time. It may be that the soul does not gain what it longs for in one incarnation, but will eventually. It is better not to rebel!

We think that by now you will begin to glimpse the enormous scope of the lessons to be learnt as the spirit journeys from its first birthplace, the heart of God, down the arc. Initially it passes through all the inner or invisible planes, to manifest at length on the lowest plane of matter. Here it evolves through the mineral, the vegetable, and animal kingdoms to the human. After, it returns on the higher arc, through higher planes in which even grander initiations are taken. At the moment, we are not concerned with these, except to say one thing. You should bear in mind that as you unfold there comes an indescribable and indefinable joy to the spirit—and there are more and more of these wonderful experiences to come. They continue until each human spirit stands forth a perfect Son–Daughter of God.

The Way is Opened

Jesus, the great Initiate, knew for many incarnations where his destiny lay. He was born on earth, but he had been long prepared as a vehicle through which the bearer of the Christ

Light could work, could find expression—not only through his mission of three years, which is but a small part of the baptism which came to the earth plane through the vehicle of the Nazarene. For with the coming of the bearer of the Christ Light functioning through Jesus of Nazareth, there came a tremendous baptism of humanity; and from that time dates the change from the old racial and tribal spirit towards the new spirit of love and peace and brotherhood.

When the light was released, as it were, from the vehicle of Jesus of Nazareth at the time of the Crucifixion, the way was opened for all people to enter the path of initiation. The symbolism of the rending of the veil in the Temple meant that the Holy of Holies which hitherto had been kept away from the common people was now open to all; that darkness which then fell on the earth, was not darkness as you understand it. Rather, the shadowed earth became dark compared with the glory of the Christ Light.

Trace the sayings of the Master; through all his teaching he emphasized that his coming would bring not that possessive personal love the individual knows, but the universal love for the whole. In the process there is bound to be confusion and suffering. Do not think that impersonal love is cold, for it is the most beautiful enfolding and healing and compassionate love of all—even as Christ revealed.

From the personal to the universal, thus humanity evolves: from race and tribe to the universal. You begin to feel brother–sisterhood, not only with all humans, but with all nature, all creation. 'Who is my brother?'—did He not say that? 'Who is my sister, my mother?' *'He that* *doeth the will of my Father which is in heaven.'**

'Those who are ready to be saved....' These are words which in the present day are cast aside but become vivid in the light of the teaching of reincarnation and karma. In truth, one must work out one's karma; but when the soul sees and comprehends the Christ Light, of itself it becomes a bearer, by that mystical contact which it makes with the love of Christ.

Letting Go and Letting God

It is true that wisdom comes from heaven as the result of your reaching upward to higher planes of heavenly understanding; and wisdom says that bitter and painful experiences grow more painful if you allow them to disturb you emotionally and mentally. You all have to learn to lay them on one side. You have to learn to forget everything except the love of the Son of God. You can think of the Son of God as pure light and love. Against this, there is always the downward pull of the lower mind and emotions, and all the physical vibrations, not only your own but those of other people in your environment.

You want to know truth; and you want to aspire and so attain a degree of control over your weaker self. This control has to be applied both upon the lowest and upon the highest plane. A cosmic law that penetrates all planes of conscious life says that all of human nature must be brought into abeyance and controlled. This you are learning very slowly and painfully on the earth plane. Presently

*Matthew 7 : 21.

there will come a time of release, when you will dwell in a state of supreme bliss and happiness, a quiescent state. On this earthly plane, however, you are in the arena, battling with forces of which at present you have little knowledge. We do not wish to frighten you, and indeed there is nothing to fear, especially when you are attached to the centre, the perfect jewel, the Christ Heart.

We see many troubled hearts and confused thoughts. But this confusion will fall away if you make the effort to contact the Divine Heart. How do we do this? By simple prayer, faith, trust, and most of all by humility. The one who is sincerely humble, who can prostrate him- or herself before the blazing throne of love, will instantly be raised up into the light; and peace will possess that person. He or she will then have touched the heart of the great Silence; and all is well when once you have perceived this.

Jesus demonstrated this truth on a number of occasions, such as when he commanded the waves to be still. All the emotions of your own troubled self will likewise become quieted when the Master takes possession of your heart. Let all your troubles fall away; because, you see, God will handle them if you will only give Him–Her the chance. God will handle them, through you and others.

We are speaking of the Master Jesus, because his is the human love and understanding that humans need, and God manifests in him. God manifests in all human beings, and to the highest degree did so in Jesus the Christ. Christ is the Solar Logos, or the Sun, and the heavenly light and life manifests through that Sun. Without the

Sun, even on the physical plane there would be no life.

Remember that God will not fail you if you do not fail God. Surrender to God's will and love and all fears will leave you. All the knotty problems will be untied. God uses His–Her children in the outworking of the divine plan, so let God's will be done in your life. Look for the God-manifestation in those who are brought into contact with you through your karma.

Of course, we know that in your world you have to submit to the impingement of other people's vibrations and thoughts. These affect you more than you realize, particularly in a big city. But you are placed where you are because it is there that your karma has brought you, and also brought to you the opportunities of which we have been speaking. When through experience you have gained control of your emotions and your thought-world, you are protected from thought-forces at a lower level.

We ask you to accept what we say. This is the spiritual law, and when there are happenings that you cannot understand, you must learn to accept them as being the result of the working-out of a law. Remember also that the earth periodically receives demonstrations indicating that if humanity, in its search for knowledge, interferes with natural law, then there are bound to be repercussions. There is a price to pay for this age of scientific experiment and research, but any lives that are sacrificed in the process are not sacrificed in vain.*

*White Eagle means in natural disasters and events that arise from lack of human wisdom, e.g. in environmental issues or the care of animals.

Sometimes people suffer and are very sad. Their lives appear to be broken up and in a state of darkness, but it is not lasting. The condition passes, and those who are suffering gradually undergo a process of spiritual expansion. With this there comes a light, a joy and a beauty hitherto unknown. Yes, life grows beautiful when you search for the beauty of God in every incident right through life.

We would tell you that you must work patiently and steadfastly towards this spiritual awakening and development. No, it is not an easy path. But as we said, the quality of thankfulness, of thankfulness to God, illumines it. So pray, my brothers and sisters, that you may learn to accept the will of God, knowing that God's purposes, although hidden from you at present, are good and wise. Pray that you may learn to accept, and pray to *will the Will of God*. What may seem bitter sorrow to you at first will in due time be revealed as a great opportunity, because through your disappointment, through your sorrow, the seed of the spiritual harvest will have been sown.

Therefore be of good cheer. Be hopeful and brave; look up into the heavens! Never look down into the slough, into the dark marshes of materialism. Look up into the golden hills, the golden kingdom of God, for this is the source of your strength. And not only your strength, for by your aspiration you will be raising all who dwell in the marshes, in the country of darkness. It means effort, we know, but we also know the reward that will be yours as you strive to look up to the light, to the kingdom of God.

VII

The Law of Correspondences

Following the Master

THE LAW of correspondences is called by some the law of harmony. It is the law by which the human soul reflects itself upon the finer ethers, upon the astral plane of desires and emotions. The conditions on the astral, the mental, and the spiritual planes are the soul-reflections that the soul's life on earth throws upon the invisible planes. 'As above, so below; as below, so above' is how the saying goes. Therefore, when the soul seeks divine illumination and endeavours to express the qualities of God, it is reflecting the heavenly into everyday life. You cannot fail to recognize the saint or elder being, because the light within such a one is a reflection from the heavens. Like always reflects like.

Let us think of the life of the Master, Jesus of Nazareth. Some believe that the portrayal of that beautiful life is merely an ideal. They consider it likely that Jesus never actually lived; and it is certainly true that so much mystery surrounds his life it is questionable whether the story as related in the four gospels is reliable—after so many teachers and translators have handled the original records. But we would have you bear in mind that whatever the historical truth, in the life of the Christian Master is portrayed the life of 'Everyman': the path of evolution which awaits every soul. Thus we put it to you that the presentation of Christ's life is a bringing down to earth of an ideal, or a spiritual man–woman of the heavens. Thus, step by step, may be traced in the birth, the initiations and the crucifixion, the exact path to be followed by the individual soul.

You will see now why we are able to say that God has already manifested in many Christed ones, not just in Jesus. But Jesus was prepared, long before he came to the earth, to be a perfect channel for the manifestation of the life of the Son of God. The life of Jesus the Christ was the most wonderful manifestation that has yet taken place on the earth planet, and the most wonderful demonstration that men and women do not die. Many stories, false as well as true, have been told about the burial or rather entombing of Jesus. But there is only one truth, and this each has to find. It lies within his or her own being.

The truth about the tomb of Jesus is illustrated by analogy with the spirit, entombed in each person's outer self and body. We do not say that this is the only entombing of the Son of God, but it is one illustration of truth; for within you and within all human kind lies the divine spirit, the Son, the light which is the saviour, the redeemer of all. In the story of the entombment of Jesus, there is a wonderful esoteric truth, one that was 'earthed' for humanity after the body's removal from the cross. His body was laid in the tomb; but where was Jesus himself? He certainly was not in that tomb. He had released himself from prison. He had become active in another sphere of life; he was active in visiting the distressed souls on the astral plane, souls who were bound down by their own follies, sin and ignorance. Sin and ignorance bind the soul. It is only love and light which lets the soul go free, and Jesus therefore ministered to those imprisoned in sin and ignorance.

As we have said, 'as above, so below'. Divine truth is being enacted all the time on the physical plane, within each human being, and also in all the events of human life. So, when you have the key, you will read divine truth into these events.

Jesus once said, *He that believeth on me, the works that I do shall he do also*.* Now, what were these works? Jesus possessed a miraculous power of healing; he could also raise the dead to life. He could give the most profound and beautiful truths to humanity in his parables. At the end, he refused to save himself from crucifixion although he had power to do so, because he still had a work to do. That work was to demonstrate to human kind that they cannot be killed, even by crucifixion, even by murder. Jesus demonstrated this, and more. But what does *the works that I do shall he do also* mean? We will tell you. In men and women dwell latent powers which, when developed, can enable them to do all sorts of things, even to leave their bodies at will and, while retaining full consciousness, travel to higher spheres. This procedure becomes normal and natural to a one whom you may call a master, or to a disciple of a master; so that

*John 14 :12.

when the physical body has served its purpose, he or she can lay it down and go on into another world—one that the great being is already accustomed to visiting.

A master can at all times move freely in the spirit world. He or she does not know death. It does not exist. But Jesus went a step beyond this, journeying to and fro between worlds. He was able so to change the atoms of his body by spiritual power, or the power of God, that his very body became transmuted, translated from dense flesh to a more etherealized or spiritualized state. Other advanced souls—not only of this earth but on other planets—who have achieved a similar degree of mastership are able, as Jesus was, to change the actual physical atom.

To follow that light is the way to freedom from all limitations of the flesh. This is how the Masters perform their miracles. They become saintlike in life. They dwell continually upon the thought of God, the purity of God, the love of God. They live in it. They absorb it. It comes to them and it goes from them. They become illumined. A saint is recognized by his or her aura and the illumination which shines from the body. You will know that a saint's body becomes so pure that it does not decay. Even that phenomenon signifies only a degree of spiritual attainment if later development does not follow. The body may not only retain its purity and its perfection, but will rise into the air and disappear from mortal sight. You know that what we tell you is true because the Master Jesus demonstrated this fact, as others have done before and since. You have the record in your Bible of Elijah, who was caught up in the chariot of fire. His body became so raised and its atoms so full of light that he went up in his chariot of fire and was illumined.

The eventual result of the soul's life upon this plane will be that after repeated incarnations and trials in a state of darkness, it will eventually come into a state of light. Entering into light, the whole body of that being will become one of light. He or she will not die, and the body will not decay as it does today. It will just be trans-ported from one state into another state, which is light and spiritual loveliness. When the body dies, the atoms decay. Of course: this follows because the truth that the body is composed entirely of light is not followed. The pull of the earth is such that the spirit in time is forced to withdraw from the body. It goes to a state of rest. Later it has another try.

You may try to seek relief from the hardships of your life, but you must not seek to escape from life except to make a stronger contact with God. Let God's light so suffuse your being that you are raised from darkness to light, from earth to heaven.

Perfect Light—Above and Below...

All life is one, and there is this interpenetration of life from above to below. But the human being, a spark from God, has to learn this by undergoing experience in the densest form of manifestation on the earth; because, remember, he—she was created to become master of matter. Yet even at the physical level, he–she is still part of the Creator; he–she is a son or daughter of God. All creation—natural, human, angelic, all forms of life—is of the one Spirit, and all are one great family with God their Father, and the Divine Mother. This mystical truth is expressed in the Holy Trinity and symbolized by the triangle. The final goal of the human life is reunion into the Holy Family, or the blessed Trinity of Father, Mother and Child. In other words, the spark of life breathed forth from the heart of the Creator travels far to incarnate in Earth. It there gains wisdom and understanding, and eventually returns with a full consciousness of itself as part of God.

The universe is created perfect. The laws governing mineral, plant, animal, and human life are exact and perfect, and all are interrelated. There is no separation between any of them. There can be no such thing as isolation in any human life. *As above, so below*; the laws relating to the spiritual life interpenetrate the physical life, and you hold within your higher consciousness a deep wisdom born of these laws, the fruit of past sowing and reaping. The crux lies in the fact that people in general have yet to attain the power to bring into physical consciousness (as Jesus did) the divine laws that govern all life. Many question us, saying, 'Why need we come back, having once tasted the glories of the heaven world? Need we soil our purity by rebirth?'. We answer that it is because you—in your greater self above—having learnt something of life's purpose, now know within that the human being, created in the image of God, must learn to bring forth into outward manifestation the divine consciousness. Even as God the Father–Mother brought into manifestation the flowers, the trees, the stars, the earth, the solar system, and the human soul, so also must God's creation, man and woman, foster that soul. You are now as children, but you are also gods in the making!

It is of the utmost importance that everyone should realize the immortal truth of the light. It is the Star that lights every man and woman on the journey homeward, heavenward. No-one can depend on anyone else to save him or her from the results of selfwill and self-indulgence. This means that the real way for men and women to acquire knowledge is not only by study of history, science and religion outside themselves, but by study of the human being, of the subject's own life, their own experiences, their own reactions to everything that happens to them in daily life. As we have said, the ancients taught that man–woman was spirit, here on earth in a physical body in order to develop consciousness of his or her own true nature, to develop consciousness of God. Thus he or she may feel and respond to that relationship from within the individual being. The microcosm can recognize relationship with the Macrocosm, the Infinite and Eternal.

We picture the Macrocosm, the Creator ever watching over every one of His–Her creatures on earth, ever watching over all creatures in every kingdom of the earth: mineral, vegetable, animal, human and divine.

VIII
The Law of Equilibrium

Working for Harmony

THE LAW of equilibrium is the law of perfect balance and supreme justice in human life: the balancing of all apparent injustice and pain with corresponding happiness. There is always a joy to come, corresponding to any measure of suffering endured rightly. When you are called upon by the law of karma to endure pain and suffering, remember that there is another law, that of compensation or equilibrium, and that this is a discipline which is preparing you to realize and enjoy a richer happiness as a compensation, a happiness you cannot achieve without mastery of the lower nature.

You cannot force the gates of heaven. There is an ordered path that every soul must tread. But although you may have to pass through unpleasant conditions, the law of compensation is always at work, for God never takes away without giving something in return. Men and women should try to recognize this law, which is constantly operating to help them in their daily lives.

Imagine the law of equilibrium like this: at one end of the pendulum, sweetness; at the other, bitterness; at the one, pain; the other, joy. There is always the rhythmic swing. And once men and women realize this, they can meet fate with a placid spirit: never regretting, and always ready to learn from experience.

In the beginning, the child is as a babe, innocent of divine law, without experience. Exactly as a child has to learn how to sit, feed, stand, walk and play, and then how to develop its brain and learn certain facts about life, so by an exactly comparable process, the spirit grows from babe to spiritual man- or womanhood. This young child in the beginning, albeit innocent, has within itself the dual aspects, called good and evil; it is expressing both what is called 'evil' and what is called 'good', and is creating a 'balance sheet' in the heavens. All souls accumulate both debts and credits. The purpose of life is to learn balance, equilibrium; and, as we have already stated, the outworking of God's law gives human kind experience, enabling it to enjoy all the gifts of the God-nature. Think about this, and then realize how much better it is to follow the path of self-discipline and strive towards God. Do not allow the forces of self-destruction to keep on crushing down your better self. The Son–Daughter of God within is building, creating, creating good—and then Cain comes and wipes it out and puts an item on the liability side of the balance sheet.

An initiate is one who has attained perfect balance, and has harmonized the two extremes, these two opposites in life. That is why the six-pointed Star, composed of two perfectly-balanced triangles, is indicative of the perfect being, the soul who has found the light and attained to a high degree of equilibrium.

Until the spirit within understands the law of God and puts this law into operation, the whole being is unbalanced; the individual lacks ease and peace of mind. He or she is in the thraldom of emotional and mental conflict, and has not attained a degree of self-discipline. How do you think the adepts, the initiates, retain a physical body long, long after the recognized human lifespan? How do they retain their youthful appearance? How can they wield that power which demonstrates their complete control over the physical atom? Only because, through a long span of many incarnations, and by practising the divine laws of life, they have achieved mastery. They are able to manipulate and control matter on all planes. When a soul understands spiritual science (which is wholly superior to physical science) then it is able to perform what to the ignorant is a miracle.

Equilibrium Works in all Areas of Life

You will wonder what all this has to do with you personally, and may say, 'But we are very far from being adepts, very far from understanding the divine law which controls matter'. Yes, but the reason we say these things is to open your minds to your infinite possibilities and the infinite power within you. The God in you will only be developed and brought through to full capacity by your own effort.

This law of equilibrium applies on all planes of life,

from the lowest to the highest. It governs all creation and every aspect of human nature. Until you can retain balance in your own life you will tend to go from one extreme to another. Eventually, through learning slowly and painfully on the earth plane, you will attain perfect control. Jesus demonstrated this truth on a number of occasions. Perhaps the most notable, as we said earlier, was when he commanded the waves to be still; all the emotions of your own troubled self will likewise become quieted when the Master takes possession of your heart.

Some of you grieve because you have lost the physical presence of a dearly-loved relative or friend, and you feel little cause for thankfulness to God. To you particularly we would say, in the words of your poet, 'God moves in a mysterious way His wonders to perform'.* Also, God never takes away without giving. If you have lost the companionship of someone dear to you, remember that God has planted within you the seed of the tree of life. The tree is within, and is the greatest gift that God has planted in His–Her eternal garden of life. What is this tree of life? The tree of life planted within you is the power, the spiritual essence by which you as an individual soul can become awakened to the heavenly worlds, the vast etheric kingdom all around you. As this tree of life develops within you, you are no longer separated from those you love who have left the physical body. You are only ever separated from them through ignorance and lack of the development of those powers, or the fruits of the tree of life.

*The eighteenth-century English poet William Cowper.

Another set of questions we are often asked is, 'What about those who are starving? What is going to happen when the planet becomes too overcrowded? How is everyone going to live?'. We answer that your Heavenly Father–Mother knows the need of all human kind. One thing is absolutely certain. The law of balance must right all problems. Humanity must do its best. Then God sees to the rest. The law, the cosmic law, which is the only law, will take over and guide and bring to you at the right time perfect balance in life upon this planet.

Many of the ills that still exist on your earth will be mitigated when there is true partnership and mutual respect between male and female. There must be equality, spiritual and mental equality. We see everywhere signs of the coming of the light in greater degree to humanity. We see this in the stimulation of the Mother aspect, or the feminine aspect of life. Women have the vision, and are beginning to take their proper place in order to bring about a more perfect balance in the world. For there comes a time when the soul has to learn and understand the law of equilibrium. Until man and woman live in perfect partnership, each playing their part in the evolution of the race, there cannot be real progress. With the arising of the feminine aspect and the balancing of life there will be great progress on your earth.

When the law of brotherhood and love is broken, always there must come the swing of the pendulum. When you see oppression, it is only temporary. The pendulum must swing back again and strike the oppressor. This is the law. At times you witness, very clearly, the swing, the rebound, of the pendulum. But the forces of destruction or evil have their part to play in the spiritual evolution of human kind. They keep the balance, as it were. It is when the scales are over-weighted on one side or the other that there is trouble. No individual can hurt his brother or her sister and escape that very hurt which he or she has inflicted. For as a man, a woman, a nation, or a race, inflicts suffering, in exactly the same measure that suffering returns. This law of balance, equilibrium, is an exact and perfect cosmic law. This does not mean that you or another person is in a position to judge the actions of a third party, but we know that the law is bound to operate. All that is required of you is trust and a loving attitude. Therefore your particular work in life as well as ours is to go about shedding love, comforting those who mourn and are sorrowful, giving encouragement and inspiration.

IX
Above All, the Law of Love

The Secret of Freedom from Rebirth

THE GREAT thing you always need to remember is that the supreme law of love rules, above all and through all. There is *always*, could you but see it, that loving care and watchfulness which guides and helps the ship into harbour. All is well. That which lies before you is for your ultimate good, because although you have created conditions that may mean suffering or may mean joy, the ultimate is perfection and union with the Beloved.

Do not worry about external events in this day of life, but concern yourself with sending forth, from your innermost, vibrations of love and beauty to create the future. Today is important only in so far as your reaction to its events creates for the future growth and harmony.

You can give love in very simple ways; by the gentle word or smile, the kindly touch, the comfort which can be offered to everyone you meet on life's journey—because every human being needs love. Is it not a wonderful law and provision of God, that God provides every one of His–Her children with the opportunity and the means to give the divine quality of love to their companions on life's way?

Therefore what your companions suffer is your personal concern. *Am I my brother's keeper?** 'Yes, indeed!'. So taught the Christed One, speaking through a man made physically and spiritually perfect. You are indeed your brother's keeper, your sister's keeper; therefore it behoves every individual to respond to and feel concern for all suffering pain. True, it is not often easy, nor always possible for you completely to change material conditions on the physical level. In the world of thought and feeling, however, you can do your part to help your companions towards the light, towards understanding of the overriding divine law, which governs all life.

If the soul can express love, learning its lesson through love, it is certainly opening and growing to God. But karma is actually created through ignorance.

In the world today, every effort is being made (though it is obscured) to return to the law of brotherhood. Love is gradually seeping in. The will to sheathe the sword is there; the wound is being healed; the kingdom of love is being restored.

None of us gets away from the law. We, you who are in incarnation, we are all responsible—a very grave thought—to a degree for our brother and sister; because our response to the good is going to help our companion to respond to good. Our lack of response, our laziness and our apathy towards spiritual things, has let the world down. The Master said, *And I, if I be lifted up from the earth, will draw all men unto me.*† This means that every individual

*Cain's remark about the slain Abel in Genesis 4 : 9. †John 12 : 32.

is responsible to some degree for the suffering, darkness and crime in the world. You may not like it, but it is so.

Ye cannot serve God and mammon.* It is so, so true. That, my beloved ones, is what we are endeavouring to impart. Once the soul in incarnation has seen the true way, that soul has a grave responsibility towards the rest of human kind. We cannot speak too earnestly on this subject. We do not preach to you, beloved brethren. We are only speaking of those things we have seen, which we have proved; and the radiation of the light in your own lives, and the establishment of centres of light, is of the greatest importance to the rest of human kind. It is *the* foremost work in the world at the present time. You and we carry a grave responsibility—and yet what a privilege, what an opportunity have we earned, so to work for the light that all beings may be illumined by the truth of the simple, spiritual revelations of the Christ!

The more this subject is studied and understood, the more the conviction grows that the *only* way—the key to *all* action on earth—is love, is kindness, gentleness. We know how right it seems to be to inflict punishment on the guilty, but the punishment is not to the flesh. The real punishment, or shall we say the lesson, is to the soul. That will come to the soul in course of time by the cosmic law, the law of God. Therefore the way of life is to be restrained, to be kind, and to have faith in the love and justice of God. *I will repay, saith the Lord*.† The law of God is absolutely just, and when a person seems to suffer

*Matthew 6 : 24. †Romans 12 : 19.

from injustice it is because of something that soul has once inflicted. It is its own action coming back upon itself.

Only through continual suffering and falling by the wayside, does a soul at last recognize the one vital truth, which is to live by the law of love. You have all embarked on the spiritual path. This means that you know the law of love; you know that it is just, perfect and true. You know that you must put it into operation, and this despite human weakness, the pull from evil, from the lower self, from the self that is created out of the dust of the earth. Everyone who lives on the physical plane has to endure this pull. This is why you must be patient and understanding with your brother or sister. Do not think or say, 'This has happened because of that person's karma; she or he must therefore suffer'. It is true that it may be due to their karma when an individual is placed in bad conditions, but it does not help him or her to be told so. Instead, you as his sister or as her brother should give sympathy, understanding and loving help. This is what God does for you, remember. This is what the messengers from the heaven world do to you. They gather round you, bringing you love, and doing whatever they are permitted to do in order to help you.

Love of Nature

The spiritual path consists of ways of service to relieve suffering, to help younger brethren towards harmony and happiness, towards Christ, the ultimate goal of every soul! The path is very difficult to find; and being found, very difficult to walk steadfastly, because there is so much to cloud the vision. The only way to maintain a foothold and to progress is not by taking up this or that path, but by entering the chamber within: by praying, with all one's strength, to the wisdom of God. When light comes, it will be not the light of intellect alone, but a light that urges the soul to love all.

Immersed in the entanglements of mind and body, how is one to find this inner light? How can you be sure that you have found the light? One thing is essential: purity of life. And here we have many problems to solve. What do we mean by purity of life? Asceticism?—a withdrawal from contact with all worldliness? Not so. You have reached the next spiral on the path of evolution, and the aspirant today is not concerned with the monastic or ascetic life of old. He or she is called to mingle with humanity: to mingle with, and bring through into the minds of those he or she meets, the light of the ages. This same light must burn brightly in the aspirant, that its influence may send healing among men and women.

Purity of the vehicles the spirit is using is one of the necessities if you would serve humanity. We are not advising drastic changes in your habits, but think about this, as well as of the human brotherhood: brotherhood with the animal kingdom! If you love the creatures given life by God, it is impossible to be cruel, to slay wantonly, indeed to shed their blood except in cases of sheer necessity. Then they are serving *you* in the only way they can serve, by giving up life itself. But with so many healthful and pure foods as an alternative, is it necessary to eat your brother or sister animal?

One form of service is to spread the light of love towards the animal kingdom: not aggressively, but gently; by thought and by example. It is not enough to say, 'I cannot bear to witness cruelty!'. You must set about doing your part in some simple way, influenced from within, to contribute harmony and love. Refuse to accept with complacency the habits and customs with which men and women exploit the weak and helpless.

By serving all the realms of creation—mineral, vegetable, animal, human, etheric, and angelic—you are in fact serving each other. And when you serve each other, that service comes back in some form. This is divine law. You cannot do good to others without doing good to yourself; but the motive behind that service is all-important. You do not serve your brother or sister in order to get something back for yourself: you serve creation and humanity because within your heart dwells tenderness, pity and love towards all life.

Wanting to Love and to be Loved…

We look forward, then, to the next step, symbolized by the flaming heart of love, the heart afire with the love of Christ. On this path of love there are still many snares and delusions. We start off with a great desire to give love, to love all … and perhaps with a sneaking desire also to be loved, which is so natural and human! Dear ones, if you learn this lesson of love yourself, there will be no question of not being loved, because the growth of that flaming heart in your own breast will give you all the love that you can possibly receive. You don't need to *want* to be loved. All you need is to love. And as soon as this is realized by the pupil, peace comes.

You may ask whether you should not endeavour to control love? Some people fall in and out of love many times, and each time think they have met their affinity. This is true. But they thus pass through their class at school; they are learning by these experiences. Yes, it is necessary to learn control of the emotional self; and the falling in and out of love is a means used to teach such control. Even when someone is hurt in the process, a soul has to pass through certain phases of experience. Only by mistakes can the soul learn. By pain and suffering that soul is growing, and growing pains are indeed painful.

Remember that all the qualities of the soul are manifested through the physical man or woman according to his or her degree of evolution. In the younger soul, for instance, the quality of love may manifest through violent or childish passions, uncontrolled and undisciplined, but it is still the same virtue, which is love. We have so often told you that love is the most desirable quality to be developed. Love still has to be disciplined; it has to be trained; it has to be directed to the highest point of aspiration. When it is manifesting at the lowest level, it can cause pain and suffering, pain in the physical body, pain in the emotional body, pain all through the being; but by slow degrees, by this very experience, you begin to understand the wisdom of applying this emotion in the right way.

In the beginning, the lesson is learnt through discretion, discrimination, but most of all through tolerance. You have an expression: 'Live and let live'. Apply that simple saying to everything in life, to men and women and their faults and failings, their peculiarities. If you can be tolerant towards humanity, towards individuals, you are taking a big step forward upon the path of discipline and unfoldment. As you put into operation the simple and fundamental quality of tolerance and kindness, you will find that without your being aware of it your heart begins to swell with love.

Identify with Life and with Each Other

Perhaps now you will better understand perhaps why we continually urge you not to spend too much time in reading, but to identify yourselves instead with life, with the joy and the sorrow of humanity? How can you enter into the depths of human experience unless you for some period of your experience become as the least of humanity? At some point, you must have felt the sorrow of the criminal; you must have experienced the crudities of the flesh, the craving of the alcoholic. You must know the utter despair of the outcast, and have suffered with the condemned.

No, do not be too respectable. And do not be amused when we say this! We speak of grave things. My brothers and my sisters, no-one who draws aside from degradation or suffering can yet identify with the Master. As you study the gospels with open eyes, you will see this truth continually expressed. Even at his death, so-called, Jesus was crucified between thieves; and it was the woman at the well, the woman in adultery, the publican and the sinner, with whom he identified himself.

Love, my beloved brethren: love to the very fullest, so that by love you may drink the cup to the very dregs. Love, knowing that the Son within will raise you to the Father–Mother God from whom you came. Knowing, as you then do, the life and the glory, you cannot live apart and become immersed in self. Be conscious of the increasing growth of divine wisdom, of the beauty of God within. Pray that your human experience, wherever it takes you, will bring compassion and love, until the body of earth shall die to self and be resurrected to God.

*

Experience in life is the greatest teacher. You are inclined to forget that painful experience teaches you or opens your eyes to joy—not immediately but eventually. The wise person sees that when death intervenes, and there is apparent tragedy in a family through death, eventually it is shown that there was a wise purpose in that bereavement and perhaps indirectly it was part of a path to eventual happiness for many people. Never grieve for souls who pass through the change of death, for those who come over to our world are met with love, wisdom and understanding. If they want to learn, if they want to understand, all possible help is given, in conditions of great harmony and happiness.

How vital it is for anyone on the spiritual path to learn

to look beneath the surface and into the heart of their companions!—to recognize the spirit and to try and understand the motive behind another's action, and not to assume always that the motive is unkind. We should all endeavour with human compassion and love to see the heart of the one who appears to be our enemy. All should aspire to act from the heart of truth—if we could ever remember that the motive *is* good, it would save us much suffering and pain!

So life goes ever forward, ever becoming more glorious and more beautiful. Take comfort, you who still tread the earth; you may do much to help your brother and sister, to help yourselves, by coming back to the simple truth—love. We believe that the only sin is the violation of the law of love. War, disease, greed—all are due to breaking this law, and men and women must learn by suffering to listen to the elder brethren, who from time to time restate, restate, restate, the simple truth.

The Power of Love to Heal and Change Lives

When the souls of men and women pass away from the earth, they go through a period of purification; and then pass through the Halls of Learning and Wisdom. After this, they enter what we sometimes call the Great Army of Light—that which serves humanity. There they work, doing much the same work as the Great Ones, but in very simple degree. The same pure light shines through them until the time comes when love in their heart grows strong. They say, 'I must go to my sister and my brother on earth. I must return and live in that dark world that I may help'. This is what you have all done previously, and so you have come back. Your one object is to learn how to love your God better; and to learn how to love and serve your brother and sister on earth. Never miss this opportunity you have chosen.

The very first thing that you all should do is to feel love towards someone who suffers—not to sit in judgment. Even the materialist, the hard businessman or mental scientist, may be searching for some mysterious secret of life. This secret, your soul tells you, is the simple love of Christ. All souls are at different stages of evolution. People who seem hard and materialistic, thinking only the material things of life matter, are in their own way searching; and may be just on the verge of learning something vital. Therefore it behoves you, as pupils of the Master, to give such people your loving understanding, rather than criticism and condemnation. On every occasion, without exception, only thoughts of love or compassion should go from you to these or anyone else. There are many snags and pitfalls on the path, but there is one certain, sure saviour. The name of this saviour of humanity is just … *love*: not a sentimental, weak emotion but something strong and constructive, compounded of faith, justice and wisdom, a balanced line of thought and feeling going from your heart out towards your companion beings.

How necessary it is to distinguish between love, which is wisdom, and emotionalism, which may disintegrate love! How necessary to recognize a love seeking not its own, opening wide its heart, thinking not harshly of that denomination or that sect, this sinner or that, not condemning, but accepting that, in all planes, the great scheme of God develops! Know that even in so-called 'evil' there is a purpose, for that which is called 'evil' is ever used by the Omnipotent to teach, through experience and through suffering, through the cross to the dawn, that humanity may see the Sun rising upon the New Age.

What is your protection, then, against the negative influences that surround the earth plane? A pure heart; pure loving aspirations: but not those of the lower nature, so interwoven with the desire of the lower vehicles, but rather of the Self, the true Self, the Son–Daughter of God. The Christ within seeks to serve, and takes no thought for itself. It indeed has no time to think of its own progress, its own initiations, of that splendid moment when it will at last enter the Great White Lodge. Of these it thinks not, but of how it can best serve and love those whom God sends within its orbit. Service, then, through love.

Love even affects the chemistry of the body. Right thought, God-thought, can reverse the chemistry that leads to illness. Not many people are as yet strong enough to hold fast to this love-thought or state of mind based upon true love; but those who can are surely saved.

Creating Harmony through Faith in Beauty and Peace

Many people on earth declare it inadvisable to look for beauty and ignore the ugly; and some may think that we draw too much attention to the beauty of the spiritual life and insufficiently enlarge upon the suffering and the ugliness of human life. We shall continue to present our subject in as beautiful a light as we can, believing that this best helps our brothers and sisters upon earth; believing too that the beam of light and beauty in the dark place of life is the surest, finest and best way to bring the human mind into harmony with the divine Spirit. Of what use is it to stand in a dark room and contemplate the darkness? No progress is made in that way; but if a lighted candle or lamp is brought into that room, it illumines and reveals all. So we hold fast to this point of view, concentrating on perfection in a world that seems to many to be full of darkness and suffering. But humanity must open its eyes to the vision glorious, before it can take one step forward on the path that will lead it eventually to that perfection.

Life goes on and on, ever evolving, ever unfolding. Never think that life is coming to an end. The decay you see, particularly in the autumn before the winter rest comes, is truly very lovely. Decaying things are in reality beautiful, because decay makes room for something new and more beautiful still. Remember, the leaves fall because the new life is pushing them off. Nature's decay is nature's rebirth, and with the decay of all physical things God makes new life. In order to have new things you must push the old away; the old has to withdraw or gradually be absorbed into the new. This applies to the members of humanity, as well as to nature. We hope you will try always to think in this way; even when you lose loved ones, remember that their physical form has dissolved into something new, not an unhappy state, but a new and glorious one.

*In the beginning was the Word; and the Word was with God.** Before the coming of the world, the *thought* of God created that which was created. The thought of peace and goodwill that the angels and the teachers continually send through to the earth plane comes so insistently because the teachers, the planetary lords, are endeavouring to sound the creative 'Word' of peace and unity. We ourselves see no other condition on earth but peace. Men and women live as in a dark house, truly blacked out, and cannot see that which lies close—much less the prospect to come. Lift up the blinds of your soul—that is, attune yourselves in your daily thoughts and aspirations—so that the windows of your soul, the seven centres of the soul, may become quickened: so that the soul can look forth with a clear, unhampered vision, and see all around the process of birth, of construction, of growth.

The Individual in the Whole

During the course of the twelve zodiacal 'Ages' through which human kind has to pass on its passage to union with the Father–Mother God, there are certain periods when the souls of men and women are offered the opportunity to make rapid progress. Such periods always bring additional pain, disturbance and suffering, but if humanity can hold constant to the Divine Love, then it

*John 1 : 1.

will take a big step on the evolutionary path. The present age through which you are passing is such a time* and opportunities are given to men and women and even to children to make unusual sacrifices.

Any acts of heroism of which you hear are events of paramount importance to the individual concerned, in their journey forward. But they are also important to all humanity, because no one soul can make such supreme effort without affecting the rest of humanity. However small the effect, such an event exercises an upward pull on the mass soul. Remember this when you read of these stories of heroism. It is true that ordinary men and women become heroes through some spontaneous urge that seems to overrule the lower mind. You will say that if a person took thought of the peril of his or her act, that person would not attempt the thing that might bring him or her pain and perhaps death. You must understand there is something stronger than the lower mind. Nothing less than a divine urge inspires and helps the soul to heroic action. Such an urge is like a sudden reunion with God. One could almost describe the person involved as being for the moment like a little child, confident in strength beyond its own, going forth to do the godlike act of valour and sacrifice. True, that 'child' sinks again to its mortal self, but nevertheless that very act has enabled the soul to make steep and rapid progress in its evolution.

*The teaching from which these words are taken was given during the Second World War, though White Eagle's words seem to relate more widely.

You stand at the commencement of a new age both of brotherhood and of the spirit: the new age of Aquarius, with its vast potential for destruction as well as progress. At this time, it is necessary for all people who understand the power of the light to call upon the angels of the light, and to give their allegiance to all that is good and Godlike, so that the white light may maintain the equilibrium and bring human kind into the golden age which is waiting to manifest on earth.

Humanity holds within its heart the balance. It is of vital importance that this balance between the positive and the negative should be kept. Negative thoughts can weigh the balance down too much on the dark side. Positive good thoughts are needed to maintain it as it should rightly be held in your world. Invisible beings are drawn to human kind to help forward evolution, and they take their keynote from humanity itself.

Equilibrium is the law. The downward pull of the earth and of darkness is strong, but the light can always triumph. The 'negative pull' is necessary, though. You say, 'What about all the evil in the world?', and we answer, 'Do you think for a moment that your Creator is unaware of what is happening on earth? Or that the Great White Brotherhood and the angels are indifferent?' The negative comes to balance the positive, and without the negative pull, or those two great opposing forces at work in life, there would be stagnation. Men and women, however, have been endowed with certain powers of spirit that are, or should be, paramount. The pure spirit of the Son of

God, the Christos, operating through the human mind and soul, must hold the balance in life. When these occult laws are understood, then there comes harmony, a balancing, and a give and take.

Give and take, this is the point. God knows when to give to His–Her children, and when in wisdom to withhold. If only you could cultivate that inner knowledge, that certainty that God is all good! If only you could learn to listen to the voice of the spirit in your heart, assuring you that God is all-wise and that the divine laws are for the salvation, the illumination, the glory of human kind!

We work with you for the day when there will be beauty in all aspects of life, manifest in every physical body, in every home life, in the communal life of all the people, in the service of all people towards each other. In other words, we are working for the coming of a new age of brotherhood—a community of all souls which will be lovely in its harmony and which will overcome or absorb into itself all suffering. You see, the human soul is like a great burning fire, if you could see truly the inner things of life. And the individual absorbs, he or she suffers, but also consumes that which is finished. It is transmuted in his or her soul.

*

In conclusion, we would have you think of life always as a journey. It is one that continues on and on up the mountain of endeavour until the peak is attained. On the apex shines the heavenly light by which the soul realizes, and becomes aflame with, God. Thenceforward that soul will be unaffected by sorrow or separation, holding within its being complete and supreme domination over all inharmonies of the planes of darkness. Brothers and sisters of the earth plane, such a glorious opportunity stretches before each one of you!

The trivialities of every day, the disappointments, the petty annoyances and the hurts, which you allow yourselves to receive from daily life, are all very small; but you yourselves allow them to become very big. Let them recede. Concentrate your whole being upon the love of God. Be a child of God! Surrender your selfwill to the divine will. 'My Father–Mother God which art in heaven, Oh! *hallowed* by thy Name! Thou art the one true glory. Thy will be done in every soul'. All is a question of submission and surrender of self—of taking life steadily and tranquilly. This does not mean cessation, but rather a sustained and continual effort to let the Christ light take possession of all your emotions, of your thinking and of your doing. It means your standing on one side and saying, 'Only God is great. I am nothing. All the good which has been accomplished in my life is the work of God'.